The Joy Journal

for Grown-ups

The Joy Journal for Grown-ups

50 homemade craft ideas to
inspire creativity and connection

Laura Brand

bluebird
books for life

First published 2022 by Bluebird
an imprint of Pan Macmillan
The Smithson, 6 Briset Street, London EC1M 5NR
EU representative: Macmillan Publishers Ireland Ltd, 1st Floor,
The Liffey Trust Centre, 117–126 Sheriff Street Upper,
Dublin 1, D01 YC43
Associated companies throughout the world
www.panmacmillan.com

ISBN 978-1-5290-7474-1

1 3 5 7 9 8 6 4 2

A CIP catalogue record for this book is available from the British Library.

Illustrations © Lucy Scholes, 2022
Design and typesetting: Heather Bowen

Printed and bound in Italy

Visit **www.panmacmillan.com/bluebird** to read more about all our books and to buy them.
You will also find features, author interviews and news of any author events, and you can
sign up for e-newsletters so that you're always first to hear about our new releases.

To my mum, Lesley, who was in a constant mode of creativity as I was growing up – from amazing birthday cakes, to party dresses and outfits made from scratch, and all that amazing cooking! Trying her hand at anything. She created so many special moments for our family and I'm forever grateful.

Lol x

Contents

. . . .

Foreword

· ·

I adore the spirit of Laura's books. Like so many of us, I have been on a journey to find a little more peace and much more joy in my day. To sit more, to linger more, to slow down much more. To worry less about the unimportant, and to spend more time, every day, out in nature – because we truly are nature, and time outside never fails to make me feel that bit better.

Reading an advance copy of this book – congrats Laura for another banger of a book! – gives me so much inspiration for everyday creativity. For example, it reminds me of the joy of writing and receiving a homemade card. As a godmother to five children, about 10 years ago I bought some alphabet stamps and an ink pad and made 'Welcome to the world' cards for each child. Some parents framed them for their children's bedrooms. I must go and dig out that stamp set again – it was always such a fun and satisfying thing to do.

Once I was on a retreat when we were given a large pebble and invited to write one word on it – something which we wanted much more of in our lives. My word was NATURE and it still sits on my desk. I love Laura's joyful invitation to paint a pebble, so now I plan to adorn mine using the mandala technique. I am so inspired by her idea of painting the dots to embrace a lovely rhythm to go with the flow.

This book celebrates many things that are not traditionally thought of as creative, including cooking. I started my food career about 12 years ago as a private chef for bands and actors who wanted feelgood cooking and home-cooked familiar foods while they were away on tour.

As well as wanting to cook with taste and ease as the priority, I like to cook and share recipes with my mental and physical health in mind. It's not just about what I'm cooking or the end result, it's the intention behind it and the rare chance to put my phone down and enjoy the experience of making something from scratch. The kitchen becomes a digital-free zone and that in itself is wonderful. What a relief to be disconnected and, hopefully, left alone!

At the stove, I remember that when I'm cooking, I'm honouring plants, farmers, soil, nature, Mother Earth. I also love that I connect more with my bloodline and heritage, and my mother's side of the family from the Philippines who I've sadly only met twice but I'm getting to know and bond with through their recipes.

One of the joys of making something homemade is also the chance to share it. I don't know about you, but I want more positive, inspiring news stories of people in the community using their hands (and feet) to do something for someone else – volunteers knitting blankets for premature babies, school kids painting artworks to adorn hospital wards, 'guerilla gardeners' transforming green spaces in urban environments, runners who use their jogging time to get outdoors and fetch prescriptions for the elderly, soup kitchens for the homeless and volunteers who cook for parents who don't always have the time or resources to home-cook for their families. Having moved country, house and school many times as a child and experienced long-term illness in my family, the positive moments that stand out are the homemade gifts of casseroles, curries, cakes and cookies left on our doorstep to welcome,

to commiserate, to remind us we weren't alone. 'From my heart to yours, from my hands to yours'.

I love bringing the outdoors in. I write this in the winter months, so like Laura suggests, I've got a selection of pinecones, rosemary and leaves on my table. They pleasingly distract from the pile of bills and remind me to get outside before it gets dark. There are also some clementines, walnuts in their shells and a few stunning pomegranates too. For now, they're making the table more inviting but, at the weekend, I'll turn those ruby jewel seeds into a ginger pomegranate cocktail and I'll throw the rest on top of my trifle for my post Sunday roast pud! On my summer tables, I pile any ingredients that haven't gone into the cooking or on the barbecue in the centre of the table – lemons, ripe tomatoes, little pots of basil and oregano too. It looks and smells beautiful. In under a minute, I can pretend I've got a taste of Tuscany in my East London kitchen.

I have picked up many of my thrifty and brilliantly frugal sustainable tips from my Mum – her best 'waste not want not' tip is to gather up leftover citrus peels, particularly orange and satsumas. When she's used the oven for dinner, she turns off the heat, scatters them in the oven on a tray and lets them 'cook' as the oven cools down. The glorious smell of them! No need to waste money on candles, she says!

Laura's also given me a great idea for using up my extra rosemary and all the lemon peels I have after cooking. Her 'recipe' for a heavenly homemade facial steam mix looks fantastic – quick and easy and using up what I've already got. I know I could certainly enjoy 10 minutes of that reinvigorating spa feeling to break up a busy afternoon and give me a welcome boost of energy.

I've already texted my girlfriends about Laura's brilliant idea for a craft club – we want to get together one evening next month to make a seasonal wreath. I've only ever made a wreath at Christmas but she's right: when it brings so much joy, why not have a wreath whenever you want? I just love the idea of a wreath adorning my front door, all year round, representing nature as it evolves throughout the months, cheerfully welcoming my friends and greeting me when I get home.

I'm off for a daily walk and when I'm back from the cold, I will be heating up a hearty portion of homemade soup. It's comfortingly beige because it's made up of all the root vegetables that need using up. It's JUST a vegetable soup but the act of making a simple nourishing meal, just for me, feels like I'm taking care of myself.

Last year, I promised myself to make time for more 'laptop-free lunches' during the week – better for stress, better for digestion, a chance to connect with myself for a moment. So I'll take 15 minutes, just me and my bowl, staring out of the window and enjoying my own company while resisting making another To Do list in my head! The hoovering and emails can wait, and those muddy-flecked tracksuit bottoms can happily do another day of walking without a wash. And I'm reminded to pause, take a big breath and notice all the moments of joy in this day.

Melissa Hemsley

Introduction

· ·

When I decided to write a book for adults on craft and creative connection, I knew I had to explore my own relationship with creativity and how it makes me feel. How do I get into the mood to create? Does my mood impact my choice of activity? How can I align the desire to 'do' or 'make' with a harmonious environment? What can I take from the freedom of play in childhood and apply to my life now, as an adult?

I want this book to speak to those of you who have never before thought to make a homemade gift for a friend or a beauty product for yourself; for those of you who struggle to carve out any time for yourself to create, play or try something new. I craft and create a lot because it makes me feel good, but I also appreciate the limitations we have in terms of time and resources, so I want to provide a different way of looking at 'me time', at slowing down and embracing simplicity.

I crave creative time. As a mother to two young girls and a beautifully busy home, finding time alone or time to 'be' without responsibility is near impossible, but I do realize more and more the importance of self-care (or 'soul care', as someone recently suggested to me). I don't mean self-care in the form of getting my nails or hair done; I mean thinking about what I need and who I am, then doing something to nurture that. That is why, when I do create the space for myself, I am often found attempting to garden (I am not a natural but I am learning and I adore getting soil-covered hands), drawing for quiet contemplation, designing something to exercise my imagination, investigating little things in nature, making a homemade beauty product for myself or a friend, or cooking up a hearty, seasonal soup! I do all of these things because they help me connect with my creativity, and that is what makes me feel replenished.

For me, there is a strong link between creativity and well-being, because as a person who finds it incredibly hard to just sit down and rest, I need to find outlets to re-charge and to balance my emotions.

Looking after ourselves is so important. Whether you are a single person, in a partnership, or a parent, we all need to put ourselves at the top of our list and discover what self-care means to us, then carve out enough space for it. I am very much on a journey of discovery with this myself. With ongoing back pain, I recently had to take some time to rest and evaluate the way I operate day to day, as well as my constant need for action and avoidance of being still. It certainly feels uncomfortable at first to be purging yourself of your most valued coping strategies, but I know on the other side of that is a more balanced, flowing life with the equilibrium we all deserve.

My Creative Journey

When I was at school, I was sure I wanted to be an actress, but when I reflect on those years, drama was never my favourite subject. Actually, I'd find performing nerve-wracking, and whenever I had to do something in front of a large group, I'd get red blotches on my skin. Floored by anxiety, I'd often forget lines in drama exams or plays.

In fact, when I look back, I was actually happiest when darting towards the art room as soon as the end-of-day bell rang, where I would work on marvellous (and sometimes dubious) clay creations with my art-room pals, perched on the high, paint-splattered stools, listening to the radio while chatting, creating, laughing and chatting some more. We loved this place with its atmosphere of a secret society, and I treasured the time spent working on sketchbooks or painting. I never felt the pressure of having to perform in the art room, and it was a relief.

Even though I knew it at the time to some extent, only now can I truly appreciate how important and special those art-room sessions were. All those tools and materials at the tips of our chipped-nail varnished fingers; firing things in a kiln, carving patterns into lino for print-making, painting in oils and acrylics, sketchbooks filled with charcoal-scribbled figures, cross-sections of plants in fine pencil, still life (always a bunch of grapes or an apple) and collage. Deadlines weren't necessarily met, but projects were eventually displayed for students and parents to observe, and we were mostly left to our own devices. More than anything, our precious after-school club gave us the space to be CREATIVE.

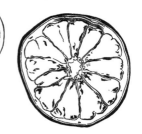

I found it very hard to concentrate or listen at school. I certainly had joie de vivre and loved a prank, adored school food (surprisingly) and was lucky to have some of the best friends I could dream of. In class, however, I chose to doodle in my folders instead of looking up at the teachers. In fact, there was one particular occasion when I was drawing something incredibly detailed in my film studies file when I was asked by the teacher to stop what I was doing and watch the film, to which I replied, without looking up, 'I'm listening.' Unfortunately for me, we were watching the (highly regarded) Japanese film *Rashomon*, which was subtitled, so either I was fluent in Japanese or a little too big for my boots (I'll let you guess which was correct!). While doodling and in the creative space generally, I was really at peace. I remember once being informed that doodling could actually help information to 'sink in', and when I had that in my armoury, there was no end to my artwork.

During my childhood, creativity wasn't only being nurtured within the four walls of the art room or on my school folders, but also at home. From a very young age, I was often seen with friends in a living-room catwalk show, bin bags strapped to us with Sellotape, mimicking, to our very best ability, high-fashion dresses, or in the garden making mud pies and crushing rose petals into water to create murky perfumes. There were second-hand sales outside our houses with painted signs inviting people to look at our wares: '20p for a lollipop' – nearly always purchased by a kind family member in the end. The innovation and determination were certainly there, and my creativity was mobilized through the trends of my youth – like bracelet making. Oh, how we

loved a bracelet swap or shop among my friends. A favourite shop of mine to go to, now sadly gone, was Helio's Fountain in the Grass Market in Edinburgh, with the most fantastic array of beads and jewellery-making tools I'd ever seen – a real wonderland for the budding creative. I'd drag my mum or gran along and stock up on clasps, tiny glass beads, faux-pearls, wooden shapes and stretchy silicone elastic using whatever pocket money I had, then I'd get to work the minute I was over the threshold of our home. Writing down in my notebook what my potential earnings might be, I really felt anything was possible; I was planning to open a hairdresser's with the money I was to make from selling those bracelets. So many ideas . . . so much joy! Do you remember what your blue-sky thinking was as a child?

It is so natural for children to find their creative flow and to experiment without being hindered by the outcome. I am interested in this and I want to guide others towards this same light-heartedness for craft and creative projects, with a great hope that it can then be implemented, even in small ways, in everyday life. And that access to it becomes much more readily available, and trying new things less scary. A good example of this would be thinking of a way of using ingredients you already have and having the confidence to create a meal with them, reducing waste, saving money and nourishing your family all at the same time. When I am in creative flow, I lose myself in a world of wonder, where I feel joy, confidence and presence, and there is no hesitation. It is not always easy to get there and sometimes it really needs to be charmed out – it certainly can't be found when I am trying to be too many things at once – but I do feel the subtle shift in mood when I just start doing, making and creating.

Joy and Play

I learned as a mother that in play and craft with my two daughters I was able to evoke that same freedom to flow, even just for a moment, if I let go of final results, if I surrendered to the moment and looked for the joy and the play within the craft or activity we were doing. This was the inspiration behind my first book, *The Joy Journal for Magical Everyday Play*. This was a compilation of mine and my daughters' favourite things to do together on rainy days, during bathtimes, in nature and to calm down, and I wrote it for other parents as much as children. I wanted to offer insight into the ways I was able to bond and connect with my girls and welcome all that comes with that, from mess and mistakes to gentle, fun play. I had given the parent's point of view considerable thought and wrote anecdotes for some of the activities to really invite readers into the ups and downs of experimenting and trying new things (and to reassure them that, yes, my daughter throws clay at the wall too or sticks her bum in the carefully arranged water sensory bowl!). I also wanted to try to find ways of making things without buying lots. This was not just for sustainability and economical reasons, but because the simplicity and limitations of some traditional recipes and ideas offered room for growth, for the individual's own input and also for so much heart. When things are pared back, it not only makes them more accessible for parents who might be short on time or resources, but also gives space for people to be themselves.

After the book came out, I was bowled over by the volume of pictures I was seeing of creations from the book . . . squishy soap, play dough, nature wands and paper bag crowns – all different, all beautiful – but it was the accompanying notes from parents that really moved me. The stories from those who were finding their flow, tapping into nostalgia for their own childhood, remembering things they had done with parents or grandparents and the re connecting to their playful side. I wanted to invite parents to unleash their creativity with total acceptance for whatever came out of it.

> **'. . . creative living is any life where a human being routinely, as an almost spiritual practice, chooses the path of curiosity over the path of fear.'**
>
> Elizabeth Gilbert, Calm Masterclass,
> 'Creative Living Beyond Fear'

I used to think the term 'creativity' only applied to artists or inventors, and to the very greatest at that. That somehow it was a term used only when a masterpiece or life changing piece of technology had been produced. It is now in adulthood that I know and embrace the fact that creativity is possible in almost everything we do, and it is in all of us, somewhere. There is creativity in cooking a meal, in getting dressed, putting on make up, brainstorming an idea in the workplace, wrapping a gift, playing with our kids, writing a note to a friend, dancing, doodling, arranging flowers, playing an instrument, problem-solving, building, being curious, taking a new path, seeing a pattern or colours in nature . . . and the list goes on.

Creativity gives us the possibility of changing a fleeting idea into an actual, physical thing. For some people this comes easily; for others it needs to be exercised regularly; and for many it may be deep, deep down and hidden beneath responsibility, fear, tiredness and overwhelm. *The Joy Journal For Grown-ups* will invite you to access that long-lost, buried ability as well as encouraging you to discover talents anew, so that you can also seek joy in craft and connect with your creative self in everyday life.

How To Use This Book

· ·

This book is an invitation to yourself. Whether you feel like crafting, relaxing, getting outdoors or gifting, there are activities and ideas here to entice you into a new form of self-care and 'me' time. They will take you through the seasons and slot into your day-to-day life with a conscious and creative approach, embracing simple pleasures and inspired by my enjoyment of all things homemade and nostalgic.

Wherever you place yourself in the world and whatever your skill set, I wanted to bring together a compendium of crafts that will appeal to everyone. For me, crafting and creative self-care is nourishing for my soul, and so I have set the activities out in a way that I hope will offer you more than just the making or doing. I hope this book prompts you to have fun, explore, gather and celebrate, and also that, beyond these pages, you will have the confidence to utilize your own unique talent and incredible imagination and take these prompts to new places – personalizing and customizing them all to suit your mood.

**'You can't use up creativity.
The more you use, the more you have.'**

Maya Angelou, from an interview
in *Bell Telephone Magazine*

I have divided the chapters up by occasion, so if you feel like capturing a moment to yourself to get swept away in the peace and quiet of making, then Chapter 1 is that invitation 'To the Self'. Thanks to some favourite kitchen-cupboard beauty products and tips, self-care treats and handy meditative craft ideas, you can use these prompts to carve out that much-needed down time.

If it's within the natural world that you seek your power, then going 'Into Nature' will be your first stop, with journalling, flower pressing or working with natural materials in new and unusual ways. Bringing the outdoors into the home is also the perfect way of honouring the seasons.

Through the unprecedented lockdowns of 2020 we have developed new rituals within our homes, for ourselves and for our families, along with new ways to mark birthdays, holidays and festivities. 'To Celebrate' is the chapter dedicated to these homemade ideas, thoughtful actions and low-cost ways of bringing that joy of an event into your lives.

There is always an opportunity to be kind and 'To Give', and with the many benefits of both craft and generosity, there is plenty of nourishment to be found in this chapter – whether you are sending something in the post or adding special touches to a gift.

The final chapter has the most unlimited potential, with prompts for how to gather with others who have a similar interest, set up craft circles and bring something new and exciting into the lives of your nearest and dearest: 'To Gather' also provides some thoughts on ice-breakers and tried-and-tested group structures that you can make your own.

At the very beginning of this book, I have included three exercises that you can use whenever you feel stuck or feel the need to slow down. They can also be used as starting points for your creative projects, because although we don't always have the opportunity to create and work on a blank canvas, within us lies so much potential for magic and originality.

Exercise: Moving Into Calm

. . . .

This is an exercise to use in gatherings or as part of your own creative self-care, when embarking on any of the projects in the book, or in your day-to-day life when you need help to connect to the world around you.

I trained as a hypnobirthing instructor after the birth of my two daughters because more than anything I wanted to share with others the amazing benefits of birth education, fear release exercises as well as breath and body work – all tools that had calmed my mind and eased my own fears during pregnancy and labour. It may seem tangential that I would be writing about this here, however, when I was recently experiencing some stress, someone said to me, 'You are living in fight or flight,' – an automatic physiological state that our bodies go into to protect us when we feel under threat. I realized then that I could use my hypnobirthing breathing techniques to rid me of unnecessary adrenalin and help me to just stop and quiet my mind for a moment.

The exercise that follows incorporates a breathing technique that I learned from my hypnobirthing teacher Hollie de Cruz; it is the first breathing technique you teach expectant mothers (and fathers) but I use it in my own life now when I experience stress or anxiety or if I need to slow down. I have combined this, for the purposes of creativity, with tuning into your senses, and I really hope you will find this as beneficial and nurturing as I do.

1. Sit in a comfortable chair. Put both of your feet on the ground and close your eyes. Be still for a moment.

2. Now, with your jaw relaxed and your mouth closed, breathe in through your nose for 4 slow counts and out through your nose for 6 slow counts. Repeat this several times.

3. Once you have got into a rhythm with your breathing and it is happening without thought, I'd like you to note how your feet feel; what is the texture, surface and temperature of the ground? Now note the sensations in your hands; if they are on your lap or on a surface, what does that feel like to touch? Next you can tune into your surroundings with your ears; what can you hear? Listen closely. Finally, open your eyes and, without moving your head, look at the colours, the light or dark spaces, the shapes and patterns around you.

4. At this point, if you want to write down your observations, feel free to do so, before carrying on with your day.

Exercise: Waking Your Creativity

. . . .

Unlocking our creativity is a strong force behind self-reflection. I won't claim that I hold the key to that (I wish I did!), but I really want to help those of you who do not know where to start, or lack the confidence to try something without the fear of making a mistake – something I know I can struggle with when I am not in a state of creative flow.

Creative flow is when you are fully immersed in any activity – whether that is performance, cooking, music or sports. Flow state puts aside any physical or emotional blocks to make way for the pure enjoyment of the 'doing'. It sounds like an amazing form of therapy to me, and I know from experience that when I am able to access this state of mind, it leaves me with positivity, energy and vibrancy that can be felt by others.

An important point to note when trying to create a flow state is that it will be easier when 'your abilities are well matched to an activity',[1] so start off by trying something achievable. Be open to new experiences, but, more importantly, be a joyful beginner.

The following exercise is really just about doodling – putting a pen or pencil in your hand and moving your hand freely for a period of time. Get yourself a clock or timer, and read on!

1. Sit in a comfortable chair and put both feet on the ground. Put on a favourite song if you like. Note your surroundings, the way the environment feels to you, and use the exercise on page 22 ('Moving Into Calm') if it calls you.

2. Set a timer for 2 minutes, then, with a piece of paper in front of you, of whatever size you wish, take a pen or pencil and put it down on the paper. Now, without taking it off the paper, start doodling – it could be a continuous line drawing, pattern making or even writing – until your timer goes off to tell you to stop.

   Note when frustration or discomfort arises. Notice the things you are led to, whether that's a repeated pattern or mark-making with no direction or symmetry. If you want to set a timer for another 2 minutes, feel free to do so, and perhaps add another colour to your page.

Once you start to feel the effects of this stirring you, relaxing your mind, helping you to think outside the box, then you can increase the time frame. While you are doing this exercise, you might find you come up with thoughts and ideas, so remember to note them down afterwards.

Exercise: Finding Inspiration

. . . .

At school, when I was struggling with learning, teachers encouraged me to use a mind map – a tool that includes a central theme, keywords and associations. I always enjoyed the doodling and colour aspects of it more than the attempts at remembering things, but amazingly I do still use mind maps when I need to organize my brain or if I am working on a project.

I am putting this into practice in this exercise to help hone thoughts and encourage originality. This can be done before starting a new activity or craft that requires you to draw, design or create pattern, and it can also be used to stimulate your creativity. I have great success with mind maps when I am looking to give my children's play and craft a new lease of life, instead of going for typical ideas (easily done), it helps me to offer them a unique and quirky direction, which is always more fun.

You will need a piece of paper or a notebook and a pen or a selection of coloured pens.

1. In the centre of the page, write a word . . . this will be your subject or theme. For the example opposite I have used autumn, as I find seasons work really well as a starting point. You can write whatever you like, though, from 'Beach' to 'Food', or even the name of a book or a favourite character.

2. From the central word, draw out 10 lines and at the ends of each branch write a word that relates to the central theme.

3. Now, for each of these new words, draw another 3 branches and write down words that come to you right away, inspired by the previous branch. Some of this will seem random and that is good. The more random, the broader and deeper you are going into the task. You can draw symbols or pictures if you feel inclined and use different colours for each branch.

4. You will now have at least 40 words written down. This is amazing. From these 40 words, narrow it down to 3. Circle them. These will guide your project.

Crafting For Calm

. . . .

A piece of research produced in Finland in 2006[2] explored the role of craft in the well-being of people who had used it as a leisure activity for years. It found that crafts as a hobby increased feelings of empowerment, personal integrity, self-expression, of learning about the self and gaining a sense of personal worth and autonomy. The article sorted craft into three different types: craft as a hobby; ordinary craft (following instructions or copying a pattern); and holistic craft (creative expression, problem-solving and self-expression). Holistic craft was found to bring deep happiness, but, in contrast, the ordinary craft (that of following instructions) was proven to help with stress management, and creating something physical could help with feelings of success and satisfaction. Craft as a hobby allows you to build new skills and can help with symptoms of depression when taken on as part of good mental health practice. In 2019, the BBC shared the results of a survey[3] in which 50,000 people took part, to find out how artistic, creative activities regulate our emotions. It noted that the reasons for people wanting to be creative were: as a distraction when suffering with their emotional well-being, self-development for self-esteem and contemplation, and to reflect and create headspace.

I hope that using this book you will find yourself tuning into your own needs and well-being, working out what it is you need. To do this, and to make the space for creative exploration, you must prioritize yourself. I hope that we can all learn to do this more often, knowing when to slow down and enjoy the endorphin rush of finding your flow.

Nature For Tonic

. . . .

By now, I am sure we are all aware of how great being outdoors and enjoying nature makes us feel and the sanctuary it provides for so many. If it wasn't for the daily walks of 2020, perhaps many of us would have struggled to find any peace of mind at all. Nature, to me, is more than just trees and birds. It is a most important antidote to our technology-driven world, and I have found in my five years as a mother that is an essential passion to pass on to our children. Re-discovering the natural world through their curiosity, excitement and joy has been a great lesson for me, and I feel very grateful that I can share some of that with you in this book. It is my wish that you too may find some joy in nature as your creativity stirs and you start to go out into the great outdoors.

There is a fantastic charity called Dose of Nature.[4] Based in London, they offer GP-referred 'green prescriptions' and encourage people to engage with nature for their mental well-being. They guide walks, sensory experiences, meditations and connecting nature crafts. There is an enormous list of benefits regarding nature's impact on mental and physical health, with the simplest and most obvious advantages being exercise and fresh air. Looking for opportunities to play, create and source materials in nature is a great way to make the most of green spaces. Discoveries will be made, and you may find a new respect and appreciation of the seasons, which can provide you with inspiration and an organic rhythm to your life.

Whatever your age, nature welcomes us with its healing, its patterns and messages, and if we can harness the enriching gifts of this great 'pick-me-up', then I believe we can all live healthier, happier and calmer lives.

Embrace Your Vulnerability

· ·

When I have done group workshops, or spoken to friends about creativity, one of the most common things I hear is, 'I am not very good at . . . ' I do it myself too. I would put my own handwriting down given the chance, but when we make these ludicrous claims of ourselves, focusing on flaws, negative characteristics and areas of shame, we are affecting our motivation and our self-confidence. This stops us in our tracks. Certainly, when we are experiencing those things, it won't feel comfortable to sign up to a class with strangers and try something new for the first time. In recent years, however, there has been so much more in the media to encourage positive self-worth, and I think it is becoming more common for us all to embrace our quirks and show our vulnerability.

> **'Vulnerability is the birthplace of love, belonging, joy, courage, empathy, and creativity. It is the source of hope, empathy, accountability, and authenticity. If we want greater clarity in our purpose or deeper and more meaningful spiritual lives, vulnerability is the path.'**
>
> Brené Brown, *Daring Greatly*

'Kintsugi' is a beautiful example of honouring faults and flaws. It is a Japanese word meaning 'to join with gold' and describes the ancient art form of mending broken pottery using gold, making no effort to disguise the cracks or breakage but, instead, recognizing the flaw and enhancing it – an exercise in appreciating the beauty in imperfection if ever there was one.

I really enjoy the way this can be applied to art and creativity for us too. Working with the 'errors' in the creation – the splat of paint, the rubbed mark or distorted image – and using them as the focus and basis on which to build the rest of the work is incredibly liberating. If we stay relaxed and open when unexpected situations arise, then we will benefit from the freedom permitted to us. It is in that freedom that we will experience growth and resilience.

Tool Box of Joy

Whether it is handy items found around the home or specific craft materials that I like to keep nearby, I want to give you a few pointers and guide you around a 'tool box of joy' that can inspire and equip you for the creative activities and prompts in this book. Hopefully it will encourage more 'doing and making' beyond these pages, when getting started seems like the biggest hurdle.

I encourage you to use what you have, keeping budget in mind and cultivating kindness towards our planet. Soon scavenging, foraging and upcycling will become second nature, and you will discover a great satisfaction that comes from that. In some cases, a craft project will benefit from a specific tool and for those I have included a list of reliable shops and online sources in the Resources section (see page 221), so you can find them with ease.

Around the Home

You will be surprised at how much you can do with what you already have. A quick raid of the kitchen or bathroom cupboard and you will find suitable tools to help when making your own beauty products, creating pieces of art or DIY decorations.

When I am looking at a recipe or activity and want to find a substitute item or alternative tool, I go through a quick checklist:

✳ What am I trying to achieve?

* What looks similar to the tool that I need? For example, a splatter guard for frying food looks like a frame used for paper making and works perfectly too.

* Is the item hygienic to use?

* Will the item wash easily? If using wax for example.

* Is the item heatproof and/or freezer-proof, if necessary?

* Can I find a more sustainable option? So instead of using lots of kitchen roll, perhaps you can dedicate a cloth or tea towel to your craft tool box.

When you start thinking in this way you become resourceful and self-sufficient – helping build confidence and self-esteem and giving a sense of achievement. It is also the economical option and will help you to think of other ways you can cut costs and become more frugal. With that in mind, here are my favourite items from around the house that will become handy when using this book:

Toilet rolls
Used wrapping paper
Old magazines
Scraps of fabric or old garments
Cardboard boxes (cut out sections and store)
Baking parchment
Deep baking trays
Silicone ice cube trays or silicone muffin moulds
Jam jars with lids
A good pair of kitchen scissors and fabric scissors

In addition to these utensils and materials, I also always have some of these things in my crafting cupboard:

Kraft labels
Air-dry clay (I use Das Clay)
Dried botanicals such as lavender, rose petals and chamomile
Wax pellets (soy or beeswax)
Good-quality round-tip paint brushes (that do not shed bristles)
Bakers' string

From Nature
Nature provides us with so much in terms of overall well-being, but there is also an abundance of materials to be found out and about. Seeking these materials becomes an activity in itself and inspiration can also be found when we are tuned into our surrounding. Nature is a great place to go when you feel creatively blocked, which is something I try to remind myself when I start to feel stuck. Read more on this in the Nature For Tonic section (see page 29).

I am going to give you a little guide to my favourite and most commonly found natural materials, but before I do, here are a few pointers on collecting and respect for the environment.

* I always try to look at the ground first to see what is fallen. You can get such a beautiful array of colours from fallen leaves in autumn and the same applies to branches or sticks: always take the deadwood.

* If you think you'd like to use a lot of herbs or lavender, perhaps you might consider potting some for yourself so you can harvest

your own. I do this and I know it will always come in handy and smell incredible!

✳ Never take too much of one thing. A good example of this is moss (used to make wreaths on page 121). You can source moss or lichen from your local florist, who will be able to acquire sheets of it. If you are foraging it from nature please only take a small amount as it is a very important part of the forest/woodland ecosystem.

✳ If you are unsure of anything or want more detail, then I have included some brilliant books and resources on nature and foraging at the back of this book (see page 221).

Have some fun finding these:

Leaves
Petals
Long grasses
Branches and sticks
Pebbles
Pinecones
Spruce
Rosemary
Wheat
Moss and lichen
Chamomile flowers
Lavender
Feathers
Shells

An Invitation . . .

To the Self

This opening chapter is an invitation for you to connect with your creativity, to try out simple, feel-good crafting and sample some homemade, nurturing recipes for self-care. I hope you will enter into the following pages in a spirit of joy, with no expectations from anyone – including yourself. If you aren't used to doing things just for you, or have never thought to get 'arts and crafty' for your own mindfulness practice, then it might feel unusual at first to find yourself in your kitchen or at your desk, slowly gathering, making and experimenting (or folding paper into the shape of a heart!), but try to embrace all of that and know that I, like you, regularly need to remind myself of the importance of doing something just for the fun of it. If you need a reminder to give yourself permission to be creative, return to the section on page 28.

You will find ten carefully chosen ideas in this chapter, from stress-relieving, grown-up play dough to an aromatic, botanical beauty treatment and a couple of paper crafts too. I love each one for a different reason, all of which I explain in my hope of enticing you to give them a go. I have kept them to a beginner level, but there is lots of room to elaborate for those who want to use these ideas as an initial prompt.

As with all the projects in this book, I have sustainability in mind where possible as well as budgets, so there won't be any need to go out and buy lots of things or embark on sourcing complex materials. My love for all things 'homespun' means a lot of the tools can be found in the kitchen cupboards or stationery drawers, and it is with that type of accessibility that I really want to welcome you all to try something new in this judgement-free, playful space.

Quick Inspiration

· ·

HOMEMADE TEA BLENDING

I want to start off by inviting you to take a moment just for yourself. So switch the phone to silent and pop the kettle on. We are going to have the most gentle of introductions as we enter into this chapter 'to the self' and look at how we can make and create with a quick inspiration to turn your next cuppa into a mindful practice.

Tea is probably my most consistent daily ritual. Every morning I come downstairs, put the kettle on (before anything else) and while it bubbles and boils I feed my herd of hungry animals. I return to place my English Breakfast tea bag and my brown sugar cube into a carefully selected mug (I have a couple of favourites that I am positive make my tea taste better) and eagerly pour in the hot water. I know exactly how long I like it to brew, and I have just enough time to go and put the family's porridge on the stove before returning to pop the milk in. Then I stop. That first sip and the comfort it brings me . . . heaven.

But it isn't just for the mornings with me. I also rely on my favourite drink when I'm tired, sad, nervous, when I'm feeling quiet, or even sociable, when I am lacking inspiration or when I'm concentrating hard, when it's cold outside, when it's hot outside, or when I just need some calm. So I get why, in Britain, we put so much weight onto this multifaceted, popular beverage.

In the spirit of 'homemade' – because this is a book on seeking joy through creative moments and crafts (and not on the origins of tea) – I want to offer you a few ways to take your own tea-drinking ritual to a new place that nurtures you, your creativity and inner alchemist as well as offering health benefits and the opportunity to slow down.

Make your own blend

Creating a tea to suit your mood is incredibly personal, which is why making your own blend with loose tea and dried botanicals is such a beautiful way to nourish yourself and soothe your soul. With that in mind, here are three ideas to try:

For a refreshing wake-up tonic
Dried peppermint, dried nettle and dried ginger

For a calming afternoon beverage
Earl Grey tea and dried lavender

For a sleepy, evening brew
Dried chamomile and dried lemon balm

Notes on tea . . .

How to make it

You can dry your own ingredients, source them from a local health-food shop or research online for good, preferably organic products. Mix together and use a teaspoon or more per 1 cup of tea. Put it into your tea strainer and brew for 3–5 minutes – if you don't have one, then put it straight into a teapot, allow to brew, then pour into your cup through a small sieve.

Make time for tea

Allocate an amount of time for this practice; take whatever time is realistic for you to fulfil the making and enjoyment of your tea.

Be mindful

Stop everything else and just do this one task, giving it your full attention. That means being in stillness while the kettle boils.

Breathe

Take slow, deep breaths while you enjoy this process and the aromas it produces.

The gift of tea

If you are making a tea as a gift, prepare your blend and put it into a clean, glass jar with a lid. Name your mix and label it, with a note on preparation.

Clay 'Flower Frog'

· ·

Before writing this segment, I had never heard of the term 'flower frog'. A small disc with holes that sits within a vase or pot or atop a jar, a flower frog makes flower arranging more of an artistic, mindful practice than a rustic gathering of blooms. It holds flowers and stems in place and is most commonly used in Japanese *'ikebana'* floral design. Here I'll show you how to make your own elegant floral offering to put on your bedside table, in your bathroom or in the entrance of your home.

What you will need
Makes 1 flower frog

Baking parchment

A ping pong ball-size piece of air-dry clay (I use Das Clay)

Rolling pin

Jam jar

Chopstick, pencil or the end of a paintbrush

Optional: Stamps for the clay or pattern-making materials, acrylic paints, waterproof varnish (I like Mod-podge)

Method
Lay out a piece of parchment on your table or whatever surface you decide to use. Work the air-dry clay for a moment in your hands to warm it up and make it more pliable. Then put it onto the parchment

and, using your rolling pin, roll it out so that the clay is larger than the opening of your chosen jar or vase. Make sure it's not too thin – about 0.5cm thickness is best.

Then, using your jar as you would a cookie cutter, press a circle out of the clay. Peel away the remaining clay from the edges and roll that up to use for another flower frog, or cover well with a food wrap or put into an air-tight container for a future project. (Well-protected, the leftover clay will last a couple of months.)

Now you have your disc, which will look like a round drinks coaster, get your chopstick, pencil or the end of a paintbrush and decide how many holes you would like in your flower frog. For a minimalist approach, you could put in 3, or, for a fuller arrangement, 7–9 holes. Then start to poke the holes through while your disc is still flat on the table. Once you've made all the holes, carefully lift the disc away from the parchment, turn it over and tidy up the underside.

If you want to make any patterns in the clay, do this now. (You'll need to do so carefully, so as not to disturb the shape of the clay too much.)

Now you are ready to let it air-dry for 24 hours. For faster results, put it into a cold oven and then turn it on to its lowest setting – around 140°C/120°C Fan/gas mark 1 – for about 2–3 hours, turning it over halfway.

I prefer to leave my flower frogs unpainted, but once dry you can of course decorate them with acrylics and coat in a waterproof varnish, which will protect the clay from any damp when used with water.

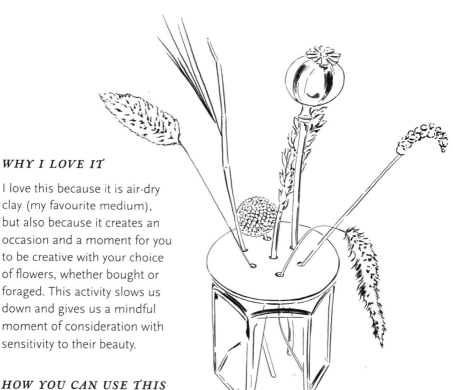

WHY I LOVE IT

I love this because it is air-dry clay (my favourite medium), but also because it creates an occasion and a moment for you to be creative with your choice of flowers, whether bought or foraged. This activity slows us down and gives us a mindful moment of consideration with sensitivity to their beauty.

HOW YOU CAN USE THIS

To use your flower frog with fresh flowers, put a little water in your jar, then place your clay disc on top. Choose your floral stems – one per hole. Cut them to different lengths; a couple of simple stems like lavender will provide contrast to a stem of fuller foliage, so when you arrange, you can do this like you are creating a piece of art, with depths, levels and charm. You can put dried flowers into the flower frog without the need for water.

MAKING IT YOUR OWN

Choose a theme for your arrangement and keep that in mind when selecting your stems. Some themes that might be a lovely starting points are:

Romance
Wild
Choose a colour
Joy

Beeswax Food Wraps

· ·

I have been using these eco-friendly, food-preserving wraps for a couple of years and they are brilliant. I have included this DIY beeswax recipe here because it is incredibly easy and will transform your food-preserving skills for life: it's a bit of kitchen self-care and certainly kinder to the planet to see your use of tinfoil and cling film reduce massively. The great thing about reusable wraps like this is that you can mould them around unusual shapes. They are also so easy to make as well as being biodegradable.

What you will need

Makes 4 small wraps or 2 large (A4 size) wraps

Fabric scissors

A3 size piece of 100% cotton fabric (washed and dried)

2 baking trays

Baking parchment

1 cup beeswax pellets (organic) (see Tip opposite)

Oven mitts

A pair of tongs

Method

Preheat the oven to 140°C/120°C Fan/gas mark 1.

Cut your fabric into whatever size you'd like, depending on what you'd like it to cover. It could be circles, squares or rectangles – you decide!

Line one baking tray with baking parchment and set aside – this is where you'll put your sheets to dry. Lay your sheets of cotton down on the second baking tray and sprinkle beeswax pellets over the top – you don't need them to be covered; just a loose sprinkling all over and right to the edges. You may need to work in batches depending on the size of your baking tray. Transfer to the oven for 3 minutes.

Use an oven mitt to take the hot tray out. If any wax is still solid, put it back in for another minute. Otherwise, put the tray on a flat surface next to your other drying tray. Using your tongs, pick one sheet up, wave it a few times back and forth to let it set, then carefully place it on the clean parchment-lined tray. Now remove your other pieces and do the same. The wax hardens very quickly so you should be able to pick these up and use them within 10 minutes.

Tip: Initially I tried to paint the melted wax on, but I destroyed a paintbrush in the process and ended up with a sheet of cotton that looked like a candle had exploded onto it, so I will not be recommending that method here!

Beeswax is much harder to clean up than soy wax but also more durable for this project. The best way I have found to remove beeswax is to reheat the wax – either briefly in the oven (if in an ovenproof vessel) or by using a little boiling water. Then, once the wax is soft, wipe it away with an old cloth. You may need to do this several times. Don't pour it down the sink, but instead soak it up in the cloth and then dispose of it. Larger areas of dried wax can be left to harden and then lifted up with a pallet knife.

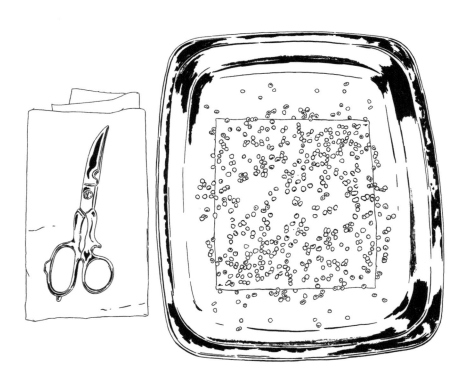

How to wash your wraps

To wash your beeswax wraps, soak them in cool, soapy water and lay them flat on a tea towel. After a few months, you will notice they don't hold so well and it might be time for a new batch. If they start to smell bad at all, dispose of them right away. Remember, they are biodegradable, so you can pop these onto the compost heap once you're done with them!

WHY I LOVE IT

Anything that moves us in the direction of less cling film is good with me. I have not completely mastered that transition in our home yet, but we try, and this is certainly helpful. For such an easy method it gives really impressive results, and I am sure you won't be able to resist passing it to your friends once you have tried it out for yourself. Beeswax also contains antibacterial properties, which makes it a great choice of wax to use here.

HOW YOU CAN USE THIS

Add these beeswax food wraps to bowls to cover a selection of fruits, vegetables, baked goods, preserves and cheeses as an alternative to cling film and tinfoil. Use butchers' string to secure if wrapping food items for a present (perhaps your Botanical Biscuits, see page 164). One thing to note: beeswax food wraps shouldn't be used on raw meat or fish.

MAKING IT YOUR OWN

This method will work on any cotton, so dig into your bag of material scraps and make some fun patterned food wraps for yourself or as a gift. Just make sure you wash the fabric first.

Scrap Fabric Twine

· ·

I imagine some of you will wonder what I'm inviting you to do here, so I will start by putting it simply. You can use scraps of fabric, twisted together in a certain way, to create your own reel of stretchy, colourful, beautiful twine. It is, like the Stress-Relieving Putty (see page 51), another twiddling exercise to busy our hands, and once you start it really is quite hard to stop. At the end of this project, you will be able to use this twine for homemade gifts, tying and decorating, and you will never let a piece of scrap fabric go to waste again. You may have seen beautiful artisan decor using this method before but, like me, never completely understood how it was achieved. I hope you will love this process as much as I do and enjoy the endless uses of Scrap Fabric Twine.

This is a really lovely way of making use of any scraps of fabric you might have. I was recently given a bag of beautiful, hand-printed material offcuts and so came across this method as a way to use them all up. You can start this with any length of fabric scraps, but they need to be roughly 2cm in width.

What you will need
Makes 1 length of twine

Fabric scraps (about 2cm in width)

Fabric scissors

Toilet-roll or kitchen-roll tube

Method

Knot 2 pieces of fabric strips together at the top. Once they are knotted, name one piece 'a' and the other piece 'b'.

Take piece 'a' and twist it tightly. Place it over piece 'b' and then twist 'b'. Cross them over again and twist 'a' before placing it over 'b' again. Twist and cross over repeatedly until you reach the end of the fabric. You can test their hold by letting go slightly and pulling; there will be an elasticity there but they shouldn't unfurl.

If you want to use lots of strips to make a long reel of twine, you need to stop around 2cm from the end of the fabric and place a new piece, 'c', overlapping one of your pieces of fabric and twisting that in before continuing the process of crossing and twisting. When you come to the end of your pieces of fabric, tie a knot and there you go!

Tip: You can pause this activity at any point by wrapping your twine around a handy kitchen- or toilet-roll tube like a reel, so you don't get in a tangle.

HOW YOU CAN USE THIS

Fabric twine can be used for so many things! You can use it to make friendship bracelets, with a loom to make a tapestry, rugs and placemats, or drinks coasters aided by a sewing machine. It can be wrapped tightly around pots to customize plants or add a personal touch to wrapping gifts.

WHY I LOVE IT

I was quite taken aback by how such a simple repurposing activity could be so satisfying and calming. I found the repeated process meditative (I was reminded of Mala beads and how the counting of each bead is used as a prompt to inhale and exhale until you have completed the round of beads on the necklace during the meditation).

I put a calming playlist on, sit comfortably and let time disappear, and while my fingers remember what they are doing, I can relax.

MAKING IT YOUR OWN

Perhaps there is a piece of clothing you are holding onto for nostalgic reasons, or maybe you love collecting beautiful fabrics but don't know what to do with them? Either way, turning them into twine will give them a new lease of life and allow you to enjoy them in an interesting way.

Stress-Relieving Putty

· ·

If you find yourself fidgeting and seeking a little self-regulation during a day of work in front of a computer, at a meeting or on a phone call, then this might be just the thing for you. I tried to think of a more innovative name for this creation, but I stuck with 'Stress-Relieving Putty' because it is exactly that. Inspired by dough-like things I've made for my children to play with, as well as the very satisfying Silly Putty of my youth, I experimented with seven different (very messy) recipes before settling on this (the least messy) one, which is made with easy-to-find, non-toxic and gentle ingredients.

What you will need

Makes 1 putty

½ cup cornflour

1 tbsp sweet almond oil

½ tbsp liquid soap

½ tsp glycerine

2 drops lavender essential oil

Jar/tin with airtight lid (sterilized and dry)

Optional: Dried lavender buds

Method

Put your cornflour into a bowl with the sweet almond oil and liquid soap and stir until it starts to form a paste. Add the glycerine and a couple of drops of lavender essential oil, then, using your hands, form the putty in the bowl before rolling it out onto a table and kneading, pressing and shaping.

Transfer to a clean jar or tin with an airtight lid. You could even sprinkle the putty with dried lavender if you like. Keep close by, ready to use.

Note: If you are pregnant, please only use essential oils if you have checked their suitability.

Which oils should I use?

The oil I used is sweet almond, but you can use other light carrier oils such as apricot or jojoba. I added the glycerine to give the putty a bouncy elasticity that you will enjoy when you press into it.

WHY I LOVE IT

As a person with a habit of restlessness and fidgeting, anything to roll around in my hand, press, squeeze and shape is a perfect tool for decompression and positive redirection. There is lots of research on why we fidget, and why one type of person is more prone to it[5] and what it might mean in terms of our attention span, but also how having a stress ball, tapping a pen, bouncing our legs or doodling can actually provide us with a type of stimulation that our body needs in order for our mind to focus better on the task at hand. Plus, the added lavender essential oil brings me immediate comfort and provides an instant calming effect.

HOW YOU CAN USE THIS

Keep it in an airtight container by your desk or in your handbag to use when you feel the need to release some stress. With the ball of putty in your hand, close your eyes, inhale 'peace' and exhale 'tension'.

MAKING IT YOUR OWN

Research calming herbs or flowers and essential oils to combine to make your own scent. Label the tin to reflect the mood you want to conjure. Perhaps try some sweet orange for a 'Happy Putty', or a 'Wake-Up' recipe that includes peppermint.

Homemade Paper

. . . .

I am sure we all use paper in some form every day, whether that is to read from, to write on, to clean up with, to carry things, to gift, to send . . . Paper really is everywhere, and although the material was first documented in China thousands of years ago, the earliest form of parchment was actually Papyrus, made in Egypt in the First Dynasty. Papyrus was a thick, material-like writing surface woven from the pith of the Papyrus plant, which is where we get the word 'paper'. If you look back to the origins of paper-making, you will begin to appreciate the labour-intensive craftsmanship of what is now an essential, mass-produced, everyday item.

I can't promise you reams of the finest, silky sheets you've ever scribbled on, but I really hope to spur your interest in this homemade, simple and rustic version. If nothing else, it will give you a good incentive to keep used paper and repurpose it with love and creativity!

What you will need

Paper scraps

Mixing bowl

Boiling water

Electric blender

Baking tray

Splatter guard (as used with frying pan)

1 spoon

1 sponge

2 tea towels

Optional: cookie-cutter shapes

Method

Tear up your scraps of paper and put them into a mixing bowl and cover with boiling water. You'll need to leave this for a minimum of 4 hours, or overnight if you prefer.

Once you return to your soaked paper, drain the water off and put the soggy sheets into an electric blender, then half-fill with clean water. Blend until it resembles a pulp. If you left the paper to soak for longer, you will be able to do this part with your hands – just keep a towel nearby to dry off!

Get your baking tray and place the splatter guard on top of it, so there is space under it to catch the water draining off.

Which paper should I use?

Brown paper bags, newspaper, wrapping paper, tissue paper, plain white paper and coloured paper all work. Bear in mind that using brown paper and heavily printed papers will darken the end colour, so if you are making the paper to write on, go for light and white papers.

Now you can either create a shape with a cookie cutter, by filling it with your pulp to about 1.5cm thickness, or you can put the pulp straight onto the guard and create a big piece that you will be able to cut out afterwards into your desired shape.

Once you have spooned your pulp onto the guard and spread it out, you need to press it down with the back of the spoon, pressing out as much water as possible. You can then take your sponge and soak water out of the paper mixture, wringing the water out of the sponge and into the sink as you go. Once you feel you have most of the water out, transfer your splatter guard onto a tea towel and continue to sponge off any excess water.

When the paper mixture starts to lift at the edges, it is ready to flip over onto your second tea towel. Take the splash guard away and leave the paper to dry for 24 hours.

When the paper has dried, you should be able to lift it off the tea towel easily. Its texture will be both soft and sturdy and it is now ready to be used for gift tags, shaped paper or notecards.

Tip: To speed things up, you can leave the paper near a radiator, but you will need to check on it to ensure it doesn't dry out too fast and crack or go too solid. Alternatively, you can also use a hairdryer on a cool setting.

HOW YOU CAN USE THIS

This paper is perfect to use as stationery, such as gift tags and notecards. Simply cut into small shapes, or use a hole punch to make your own confetti. I have also added a project on page 89 for how to add seeds and dried flowers to your paper, as a way to connect this with a love of nature.

MAKING IT YOUR OWN

Why not add a few drops of essential oil to your paper mixture and pop some pieces into your drawers to keep clothing fresh and aromatic? Lavender will also keep moths at bay! You can also add botanical or natural dyes such as beetroot juice or turmeric powder at the blending phase to create brightly coloured papers.

WHY I LOVE IT

I have always wanted to get into regular paper-making, but mistakenly thought I needed a vast array of materials in order to do so. This basic method opens up our possibilities for reusing and recycling as well as the satisfaction of having homemade paper at the end of it. I love the process and the many directions it can be taken with a little bit of experimentation and fun.

Soy Wax Melts

· ·

This is a brilliant way of repurposing candle ends, and it is also really simple and effective if making fresh with wax beads. I have chosen to use soy wax as it burns with less scent than beeswax and is much easier to clean up, but you can substitute this with the same measurements of beeswax if you want to. They make a really beautiful gift, but I have included them here in this invitation to the self because there is something so comforting about making yourself a cup of tea and lighting a candle or diffuser to scent your space and conjure some cosiness.

What you will need
Makes 12 small melts

Heatproof mixing bowl

Saucepan

5 tbsp soy wax pellets (or ends of candles)

1 tbsp coconut oil

1 tsp essential oil (or try more than one scent)

Silicone ice cube or baking tray (ones with small holes are best for this)

Measuring jug

Jam jar with lid (sterilized and dry)

Optional: 1 tsp dried flowers

Method

Set up a bain-marie by setting a heatproof mixing bowl on top of a small saucepan of water. Make sure the base of the bowl doesn't touch the water. Turn the heat on to get a rolling boil and then add the wax pellets or candle ends to the mixing bowl to melt. If you want to stir use a metal or plastic spoon, otherwise just leave it to melt.

Once the wax has melted, add the coconut oil and stir. If you are using one scent, put the essential oil in now and stir again. If you want to use a variety of scents, put a drop of essential oil into each hole of your silicone mould. You can add dried flowers at this point if you want, which looks incredibly pretty but won't necessarily give off a scent unless they are highly perfumed rose petals or similar.

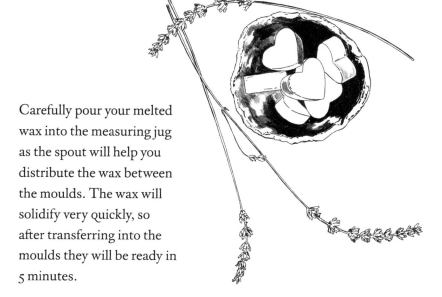

Carefully pour your melted wax into the measuring jug as the spout will help you distribute the wax between the moulds. The wax will solidify very quickly, so after transferring into the moulds they will be ready in 5 minutes.

They will melt more slowly in your burner if you let them settle for 24 hours before using, so pop them out of the moulds and into a jar to keep or give as a gift!

If you are pregnant, please only use essential oils if you have checked their suitability.

HOW YOU CAN USE THIS

I use my wax melts in a ceramic oil burner. I pop the shapes into the top well and light the candle, which will slowly melt the wax and diffuse the scent into the room. When I put the candle out, or if it burns out, the wax will harden and you can continue to use that the next time you are looking to add fragrance to your space.

When you want to clean out the diffuser, you can wait until it reaches the end of the wax and, while still warm, wipe with kitchen roll. Soy wax comes away easily with soapy water. Otherwise, pour boiling water in to soften the wax and catch the wax beads which will form on the surface with a piece of kitchen roll and dispose of the water.

WHY I LOVE IT

These wax melts seem to make the scent in an oil burner go further and using soy wax means it cleans really easily. They also look good enough to eat in their sweet, small shapes and can be popped into a clean lidded jar to make a thoughtful homemade gift.

MAKING IT YOUR OWN

You can add dried botanicals to the wax melts, and because they aren't in direct contact with a flame, they will heat with the molten wax. Lavender has a relaxing aroma and looks very beautiful.

Calming Origami Hearts

. . . .

I am on a journey of learning origami. I love it so much that I want to share it with you here and invite you to give this easy origami-style shape a try. Origami literally means 'folding paper' in Japanese and is a highly skilled craft which many feel both perplexed and daunted by – myself included. The most well-known origami structure is the paper crane, of which I'm yet to master, but here we are going to try a flat, beginner's-level paper-folding technique to create a heart. A bit like learning to drive, once I have repeated each step of the origami a few times, I start to remember it and my fingers move with more ease. My mind always feels rested and restored too, which makes this invitation particularly good for the soul.

What you will need
Makes 1 origami heart

Square piece of lightweight paper (I use an 18cm x 18cm piece)

A flat surface to work on

Method
If you are working with paper that has a design on it, then you will want to turn it over with the design face down. Working on a flat surface, take your top-right corner and fold it diagonally to the bottom left and then press the fold down in one strike of the finger.

Open the paper back out and
now take top left-hand corner
and fold that diagonally to the
bottom-right corner, then strike
your finger down the fold again.
Now unfold the paper and reveal
a cross from your two folds.

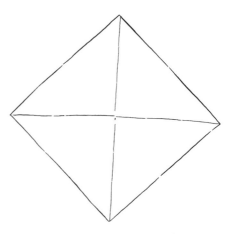

Turn the paper so that the shape
becomes a diamond and with the
top point, fold that to meet the
fold that goes centrally through
the paper. Now take the bottom
point and bring it right up to
meet the top edge.

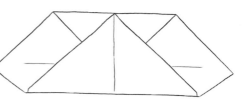

Pick up your bottom-right
straight edge and fold it
upward through the middle
(see illustration, right).
Press all your folds down
and pick up your bottom-left
straight edge and bring
that upward through the
middle. It should now be
starting to look like a very
pointy heart!

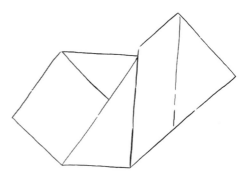

Flip your heart over and turn your top heart points down to meet the top straight edge. Now fold in the two side points. Flip it back over to see your first, simple, origami-style heart!

WHY I LOVE IT

Paper-folding is meditative and calming not only to watch but to do, in a way that took me by surprise. I thought it would be too hard to even give it a try, but I have since learned a few simple, beautiful ways to create origami shapes.

MAKING IT YOUR OWN

Stick on pressed flowers or tuck one under a fold as a little surprise. Write a message on the inside of the paper or attach delicately to thread and hang up in a window, as a floating paper mobile.

HOW YOU CAN USE THIS

I have made the heart-shaped origami into little Valentine's tokens and sent them as gift cards to friends as joyful post.

Face and Body Exfoliator

· ·

Creating my own beauty products has always been a passion. Learning from amazing books, blogs and inspiring nature-based beauticians and herbalists, I have played around with kitchen ingredients and herbs, oils and tinctures for years, enjoying the process of mixing, making and nourishing myself with the great gift of a homemade product. These simple body and face exfoliators will remove dead cells and blackheads, encourage blood circulation and lymphatic flow, and leave you glowing. I hope you will find that there is something for everyone here.

What you will need

Makes 1 jar of exfoliator

Small bowl

Tablespoon

Jam jar with lid (sterilized and dry)

For an Invigorating Face Exfoliator

¼ cup used coffee grounds

1 tbsp fine brown sugar

1 tbsp coconut oil

Optional: 4 drops rosehip oil

For a Gentle Face Exfoliator

1 cup ground oats

2 tbsp fine brown sugar

1 tbsp runny honey

2 tbsp coconut oil

Optional: 4 drops rosehip oil

For a Calming Body Exfoliator

Rolled oats (use your jar to measure)

½ cup sweet almond oil

2 tbsp dried lavender

Tips: To create a looser body exfoliator, add more oil. For a stronger exfoliator, use large brown sugar granules. You can work with the contents of a used coffee capsule for this too! To make the Invigorating Face Exfoliator into a body exfoliator, simply add more coconut oil.

Methods

For the Face Exfoliators
Add all the ingredients to a small bowl and smooth together with a spoon.

For the Calming Body Exfoliator
Half-fill a jam jar with rolled oats, add the oil and the dried lavender. Pop the lid on and shake to mix.

How to store

Keep your exfoliators in sealed jars, labelled with ingredients and the date they were made, in a dark cool place, or the fridge. If the latter, you may need to pop your jar into a bowl of warm water before using, as it will have solidified. As with anything homemade, if it starts to smell bad, do not use.

WHY I LOVE IT

This is a homemade product that really works, saves money and uses things I would have been throwing away (used coffee grounds!). I find it's one of the most satisfying and thrifty ways to enjoy self-care and DIY beauty.

MAKING IT YOUR OWN

Knowing your skin type will mean you can tailor these exfoliators to suit you exactly, and you can make them in as small or as large a quantity as you need.

HOW YOU CAN USE THIS

With the face exfoliators, wash your face and then, using two fingertips, scoop a little of the scrub out and start to rub in small circles on your forehead, cheeks, chin and jaw line. If you want to use a little under your eyes, then dab this on and leave it for 2–3 minutes before washing off with warm water and drying with a towel.

The body exfoliator is an amazing addition to the shower. Use a body brush or the palm of your hand to apply in big sweeps and circular motions around your hands, tummy and legs. You can also use this on your feet – just cover them in a good amount and massage before washing off in the bath.

Facial Steam Mix

· ·

Whether it's grabbing a moment before the family wake up to have a fresh and energizing steam or carving out some time of an evening when I need to bring myself down into a space of relaxation, a herbal facial steam is a really beautiful way to pause and reset. There is a huge variety of combinations to try, and it's so easy to set up that you only need to find 5 minutes of free time to reap the benefits of a herbal steam. Whatever ingredients you choose to include, it will be sure to hydrate, cleanse, decongest and calm. Enjoy!

What you will need

Makes 1 jar of mix

Jam jar with lid
(sterilized and dry)

Tablespoon

Large bowl

Towel

Sticky label

Pen

Optional: Baking tray

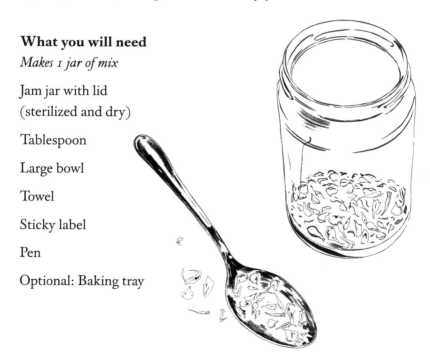

Scent Additions

Choose 2–4 of the following ingredients:

Dried rose petals (soothing, hydrating, anti-ageing)

Dried lavender (calming, good for dry skin)

Dried calendula (healing, soothing for eczema)

Dried peppermint (decongestant, awakening)

Dried chamomile (soothing, relaxing, good for blemishes and irritations)

Fresh mint (antibacterial, decongestant)

Fresh rosemary (decongestant, antiviral)

Fresh sage (clears the head, hydrating, soothing for acne)

Lemon peel (cleansing, invigorating, soothing for acne)

Pine needles (releases toxins, decongestant)

Method

For a dried herb mix:
Fill the jar with your dry ingredients, tailoring the quantities of each botanical to suit your needs. To use, put a tablespoon of mix into a large bowl, then pour 560ml of boiling water over the top. Remember to label and date any leftover mix.

For a fresh herb mix:

Pluck a few herbs, or peel 3–4 pieces from your lemon. Put the herbs into the bowl and pour 560ml of boiling water over the top. If using lemon, twist the pieces of peel to release some oils and pop them into the water.

Tip: If you want to add fresh herbs or lemon to a dry mix to give as a gift or use at a later stage, then place them spaced out on a baking tray and leave in cool, dry place to air-dry for a couple of days.

WHY I LOVE IT

Each of these blends will be unique; there are no rules about how much or little to put in, so the whole process feels bespoke. I light a candle, dim the lights and enjoy this space as a truly restorative time. I also really love that my skin glows for ages afterwards!

MAKING IT YOUR OWN

Why not turn your mix into a bath soak? Place the dried mix onto the centre of a little piece of cotton (a baby muslin works!), then simply tie it with a knot and add it to a hot bath.

HOW YOU CAN USE THIS

Keep your mix in a cool, dry place and go to it when you feel the need for a pick-me-up of a morning or to unwind at the end of the day. When you set it up, make sure you are sitting comfortably with the bowl of hot water at the correct level so that you are neither craning your neck upward or bending over too low – putting it on the kitchen table and sitting in a chair with a cushion is ideal. With your face hovering over the water and a towel over your head and the bowl, take long, slow breaths in and out for 5–10 minutes. After your facial steam, dab dry with a clean towel and moisturize.

An Invitation . . .

Into Nature

Nature offers so much, whether it is the abundant benefits to your physical health and mental well-being or your connection to the world around you. It is also a great source for creative inspiration – my favourite, actually. If you tune into and stay present in the surroundings of nature on a walk – whether it's 5 minutes down your road to a shop or a longer walk in a forest, field or on the beach – you can see and understand so much more than initially meets the eye: swirls and mandala patterns within the shell of a snail or the unfurling of a fern; the pastel blues and lime green colours of lichen engulfing an old, wooden gate post; familiar shades and hues that take us through the year – a seasonal Pantone colour chart for your surroundings.

Incorporating nature and its foraged or found materials, respectfully, into our crafting will not only connect us to this rich, nutritious and life-giving physical world around us, but it will also help us begin to honour the history of 'craft', the traditional ways of being creative and artistic, and those artisans who have been developing and sharing skills and knowledge of the natural world for thousands of years.

Whether you are inspired to string up dried posies to bring botanical fragrance into your home or make your own items of clothing and accessories with natural dyes, I hope you, like me, will find the earthly qualities of crafting with nature to be restorative and uplifting.

Quick Inspiration

. . . .

PRESSING FLOWERS

Delicate pressed flowers can be used in many crafts, from homemade cards to candles and even in baking (as you will find later in this book), but they also capture a seasonal moment in nature – one that you can savour and reflect back on weeks, months, or sometimes even years later.

Although flower presses are readily available to buy in most gift or craft shops, and can even be made easily for those with some DIY skills, I wanted to enter into this chapter with a little easy prompt to show you how to get creative using books that you already have around the home.

Some flowers are more easily pressed using a flower press thanks to the weight or tightening of screws, so, as we will be using the weight of

books to press flowers, I'd recommend daisies, pansies, honeysuckle, clovers, poppies, cornflowers, buttercups and narcissus for best results.

For this, you will just need either two pieces of kitchen roll or two pieces of baking parchment along with your heaviest hardback book and a couple of extra books too.

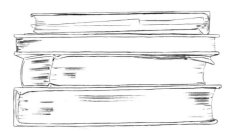

1. Go right to the back pages of the heavy book and put one piece of parchment down, then lay your flowers on top, spread out with space between them.

2. Place the other piece of parchment on top of the flowers. You can now close your book.

3. Put some other books on top and either remind yourself with a little 'note to self' or put the books somewhere memorable to avoid forgotten flowers . . . although that in itself always provides a charming surprise for the reader!

4. Your flowers will be pressed to perfection in 3–4 weeks.

Nature Journal

· ·

The idea of a nature journal is to connect you to the seasons, to the natural world around you and to start to see things differently – colours, details, patterns, shapes and rhythms . . . Beyond that, a nature journal can also provide you with a personal sanctuary for mindfulness and inspiration.

Journalling is commonly known to be a great form of self-care, as it promotes clarity of mind, helps boost our memory, process events and advance our communication skills and self-confidence.[6] I have always been quite sporadic with keeping a journal, but I love to write, make notes and have benefitted enormously from 'Morning Pages', which is an exercise from *The Artist's Way* by Julia Cameron. Unlike journalling around a theme or thought, Morning Pages are your written stream of consciousness first thing when you wake in the morning, which you complete without stopping until you've covered three sides of paper.

For me, a nature journal is a combination of a written journal – with notes, words, prompts and observations – and an artist's sketchbook, with doodles, colour swatches, pressed flowers and FUN!

What you will need

Notebook or homemade book (see page 77)

Pens, pencils or watercolour paints

Brown Kraft tape or glue stick

The outside world!

Method

Getting started will probably prove to be the trickiest part of this process, but remember there is no right or wrong. This is a completely personal, for-your-eyes-only project which you can pick up and put down as and when you feel inclined. To give you a helping hand, however, this would be my suggestion and the method I use to ease out of a creative rut.

First, on each page, write the date, your location and the time of day – these will constitute the 'log book' element of your diary. Of course, you may like to write only about one specific walk and all the different ways that walk appears to you through the year, or you may write only about your garden or balcony, but for those who have the opportunity to be in nature often and in various places, this might be a different location every time – maybe even a different country for the adventurers among us! You can also add in the weather on the day and who (if anyone) you are with.

Tip: This is perfectly suited to a solitary activity – and might be necessarily so for those with busy lives seeking this sanctuary – but it can also work as a family activity with lots of nature-spotting to occupy kids!

This is where we delve a little deeper . . . Think about how you are feeling as you open the page. It might mean giving yourself a moment to tune in. Step outside, put your book down for a moment, close your eyes and take 3 slow, deep breaths in and out. When we do this, feelings might come up. It might even be hard for us to surrender to that stillness and breath, but whatever comes up for you, whether it is an event, an emotion

or a physical feeling, note it down in a sentence or a word. I find that my mood changes in nature; I calm and slow down. My heart rate drops and I feel invigorated. If you feel inclined to note down how you feel after your walk, then you might also learn that nature is your tonic too.

The rest of the walk with your journal will be about observing and, in whatever your chosen medium, recording what you see, hear and feel. Here are some additional prompts if you need help with shaping this:

✳ Notice 1 new thing along your walk

✳ What 4 colours can you see?

* How does this season affect the trees/plants on this walk?

* How does the ground feel under your feet?

* Jot down something on the walk that remind you of your childhood/brings on nostalgia

HOW YOU CAN USE THIS

I use a nature journal as a form of mindful practice and also as my own art book, all rolled into one, so it feels very personal and interesting to look back on and reminds me of the importance of connecting to nature for my own well-being.

WHY I LOVE IT

I love the idea of tracking the natural world and watching it shape-shift through the seasons. Having my nature journal provides a beautiful reflection on this, as well as abundant opportunity for learning and fine-tuning my awareness of what is around me.

Bluebells, for example, will pop up from one day to the next and before you can even blink, your shaded forest walk is alive and glowing with the purple bells of springtime!

MAKING IT YOUR OWN

You can put your own journal together by collecting scrap paper and sandwiching the sheets between two pieces of cardboard, tied up with string . . . or you can use a journal with blank or lined pages. Not only is making your own journal the more sustainable option but it also means you will end up with something special and unique. Label and date your journal so you can reflect on it in years to come.

Painted Mandala Pebbles

· ·

I have hosted a couple of workshops where we have done this activity and those taking part told me they found it meditative, therapeutic and calming, that it felt amazing to connect with creativity and provided a space for child-like freedom.

It is admittedly a really simple activity, and although painting pebbles may feel like it should feature in a children's craft book (and, yes, I did include a version of it in *The Joy Journal for Magical Everyday Play*), there are a few ways to enhance it and create a treasured keepsake, a handy paperweight or tokens of love for a fellow human to find along their path.

When we are taking a natural material from the earth, I was once told by a beautiful friend that we should thank the earth. It may seem unusual to suggest this, but as we all grow and develop our consciousness for the planet and understanding of its requirements from us, we too can create simple gratitude rituals like a quiet 'thank you' when we watch a beautiful sunset, pick a flower, or find a rock or pebble to create with.

For this creative activity we are going to be inspired by a mandala pattern. In Sanskrit, the word mandala means 'circle', and it is typically a design or pattern of symbols and shapes radiating outward in a circle from a central point. The pattern-making is used in many spiritual traditions as a practice of focus, meditation, self-awareness and reflection.[7]

You can use a picture of a mandala sourced from the internet or a book as inspiration, draw one yourself, or perhaps use a similar circular pattern found in nature, like the swirl of a snail shell, the centre of a sunflower, a spider's web or sea urchin.

What you will need

Makes 1 painted pebble or stone

A pebble or stone (any size; the larger it is, the more space to create)

Small pot of water

Acrylic paint or outdoor acrylic paint

Paint palette/plate

A pointed-tip paintbrush

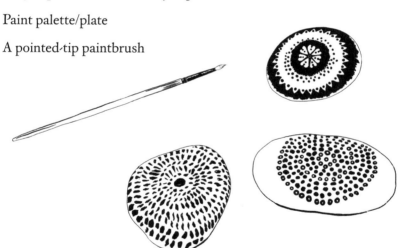

Method

Wash and dry your pebble or stone. Prepare a small pot of water, choose your paint colours and dispense them onto a palette or plate and get your pointed-tip paintbrush.

We are going to be using a dotted method. If you want to practise this on paper, dip the tip of your brush into the paint, then with one dot start to create your pattern. You don't need to return to the dot to make it perfect, or bigger; however it ends up is just right.

If you are going straight onto the pebble without a reference picture, start with your central dot, then add a dotted circle around the central point. Then, between each of those dots add your next dotted circle. This is now going to be your method going forward, and you can change your colours as you wish. If you are using a reference picture, use this same dotted method to replicate the image you are looking at.

Allow yourself to go 'off-page' with it, so if you make a mistake, embrace it and make it a feature rather than trying to cover it up.

WHY I LOVE IT

I love the method of using dots on painted projects because it really helps me shut off my analytical brain and embrace flow. There is a rhythm to it that is mesmerizing, and I feel like my inner child is always thankful for a bit of time crafting like this.

MAKING IT YOUR OWN

Beyond the dotted mandala, of course, you can create any design on your pebble. Perhaps write underneath in a white pencil or paint the date and where you found it.

HOW YOU CAN USE THIS

You could keep this for yourself, varnish it if you want to preserve it and perhaps it can make a great paperweight, ornament or welcome sign on your doorstep. Otherwise, I have seen many a painted pebble left in nature for others to find . . . a message to the world and fellow humans.

Pounded Petal Prints

· ·

Petal pounding is also known as Hapazome,[8] and is the traditional art of pounding and printing leaves and flowers onto fabric. I discovered it last summer when looking for a way I could craft with my daughters using a beautiful bunch of flowers that were on their way out. I tried it out on a tea towel and although my kids were a bit young to use a hammer, we used one of their wooden toy mallets. It had a good effect and the kids loved it, but I was very much looking forward to getting down to the real hammering business, which is why I went on to continue this craft for myself, using this very cathartic technique.

What you will need

Makes 1 printed fabric sheet

Selection of leaves, petals, grasses

Baking parchment

Fabric: cotton, calico or muslin in white or a light colour (any size)

A camping mallet or hammer

Optional: Chopping board, tea towel

Method

First we want to collect a selection of natural materials, and I found through a lot of trial and error that some leaves, petals and flowers work better than others; in fact, some don't press any colour at all. Here are

the ones I had consistent results with: clover leaves, grass, dark rose petals, golden marguerite, yellow daisies, dahlias in dark shades of pink and orange, pansies, soft green leaves, lavender and, for the more daring among us, nettles (use gloves when picking).

To protect your surface from being stained by the dyes, cover it in baking parchment. If you would rather use a chopping board for this, then put a tea towel underneath to hold it in place securely (and soften the noise slightly!).

You can now decide if you want to pluck petals or keep whole flowers, also if you want to create a pattern or if you would prefer to spread your petals and leaves around at random on the baking parchment. If you are struggling for inspiration, perhaps start with a mandala pattern (see page 78).

Once you are happy with your placement, carefully place your fabric over the top of the petals and, using your hammer, start to pound the fabric. You will quickly see coloured shapes coming through as the hammer extracts the moisture and colour from the leaves and flowers, leaving splashes of pigment behind. You don't need to do large whacks of the hammer; in fact it can be done in a very considered way, working over the whole piece of fabric, finding your own rhythm with it.

When you are happy that you have done all you can with the petal pounding, slowly lift your fabric up. There will be some petals and

leaves attached to the fabric – simply sweep these off gently with your finger or roll across them with your finger pads until they come away leaving interesting botanical shapes and splashes of colour.

WHY I LOVE IT

I absolutely love the effect of this craft and seeing the printed patterns and botanical dyes on the fabric. It is a versatile activity because you can use your printed fabric for so many things. The process of collecting your natural materials for this, in itself, connects us to nature, leading us to investigate different flora and, most of all, the wonders of natural dyes and patterns found in the natural world.

HOW YOU CAN USE THIS

This method can be used to create homemade bunting, material wrapping for an extra special touch to a gift, scarves or handkerchiefs and for much larger projects you can create stunning curtain panels and bedspreads (using a white sheet!)

MAKING IT YOUR OWN

Using a needle and thread, you can stitch into your petal-printed fabric, either a simple line stitch to add texture or follow around the edges of some of the prints.

Botanical Bundle Dye

. . . .

I became quite captivated by video tutorials of bundle dying over the past year. The process is relaxing to watch, but I can vouch that it is just as relaxing to do. There are a few different methods that use more professional materials and fine-tuned techniques, but I have opted for a short and sweet version which is still satisfying and will give you beautiful results – sort of like a very delicate, organic tie-dye. I have chosen to use silk here as it is effective in getting a vibrant end result, but you can also use cotton.

Before we start, there is a little preamble for this craft (the same applies to Pounded Petal Prints on page 81). Bright and vibrant flowers and petals won't always give you the bright, colourful effect you are seeking, and it's all to do with how much pigment the flower contains. I have found myself spending ages carefully arranging a pattern of petals and leaves onto fabric, placing each one with care . . . only to find they have almost no pigment and simply crush into a watered brown. There is a science (or rather the science of botany) behind it, but for now, just play around and have a go with a variety and see what works out for you. I have listed a few great options to start off with opposite.

What you will need

Makes 1 dyed piece of silk

A piece of silk (I used a handkerchief measuring 55cm x 55cm)

Floral selection (see Tip above)

Bakers' string

Steamer or colander, which sits on a saucepan

Tongs

Fabric scissors

Optional: Water spray

Method

Take your piece of silk (I got mine at a craft shop) and wet it all over. You can either use a water spray or put it under a cold tap for a moment, but wring out some of the water so it's not dripping.

Lay the damp silk down onto a clean, flat surface and spread your petals, leaves or whole flowers onto one half of the silk. You can do this sporadically or, like me, with a little symmetry, which creates a good effect in the dye pattern. The floral placing is the part I find most relaxing, so take a moment here to enjoy the rhythm of it.

When you're happy with
your design, fold the
other half of the silk over
the top of the flowers.

Now, starting at the fold, roll
the folded silk all the way to the
top until you have a snake (or an
uncut sushi roll), then roll this in
like a spiralling snail shell. Take
your bakers' string (I use this
type of string as it doesn't have
any colour and so doesn't effect
the colouring of the fabric) and
bind the silk roll-up and tie it off.

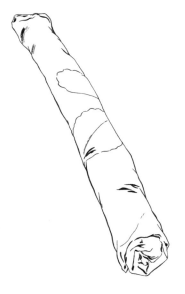

Now add water to the steamer and place the silk bundle inside. Turn your stove on and when you have a little simmer and start to see the steam, put the lid on. If you don't have a steamer, put your colander into a large pan with 2cm of water and put the lid on. Steam the bundle for 2 hours, however set a timer for 1 hour and turn it over with tongs before putting the lid back on.

When the 2 hours is up, using your tongs, take the bundle and hold it under a cold tap until it's cool enough to touch. Untie the string and release the bundle over a bowl or the sink so the flowers can fall away. Flatten out the silk and pick away the remaining bits of the flowers that are a little more stuck and give it one final rinse under water.

As your silk dries, you will notice the colours become more vibrant.

Tip: Don't leave your steamer for too long unattended – I did the first time I did this and because I hadn't put enough water in, it had boiled away and burned the bottom of my pan, which I'd have known (because of the smell) had I been in the room.

WHY I LOVE IT

I absolutely love discovering natural dyes, whether that's for creative activities with my kids or for any project I might be doing myself. It feels like the sort of gentle, crafty science that is just the right tempo for me.

HOW YOU CAN USE THIS

Using a silk square means you have a beautiful neckerchief, handkerchief or headscarf at the end of it, or, alternatively, an exquisite hand-dyed furoshiki wrap (see page 158) to use or gift to a friend.

MAKING IT YOUR OWN

I recently found a few incredible crafters who use their food waste (like onion skins, beetroot ends and carrot peels) with the same technique to produce incredible dyes and patterns. You could also try adding a sprinkle of turmeric or wheatgrass powder.

Homemade Seed Paper

· ·

Taking our newly acquired paper-making skills from the project on page 54 to the next level, here we are going to make a batch of paper with the addition of flower, vegetable or herb seeds. It makes the perfect gift for a loved one who can watch the seeds germinate and bloom.

What you will need

Ingredients for 'Homemade Paper' (see page 54)

Various seeds (see Tip on page 90)

Method

Follow the method on page 54 until you have your wet pulp on the splash guard. Spread the pulp around either using the cookie cutter to mould a shape or just freestyle on your surface. Gently pat a little water off with a cloth, pressing down slightly so some of the excess water comes through the splash guard into your baking tray. Don't allow the pulp to dry completely.

Tip the paper onto a tea towel. You can now sprinkle the seeds over the surface of the paper and pat them gently into the damp surface with a finger pad or rolling pin depending on the size of your project.

Leave the paper to set for 24 hours.

Which seeds should I use?

It is better to opt for small seeds for the seed paper as larger seeds might not embed. Vegetable seeds like those from a chilli, wheatgrass or sprouts are a good option. When placing your seeds on the paper, check whether you need to use a handful or only a few. There will be information online or on the packet about the optimal amount for each plant's specific germination needs.

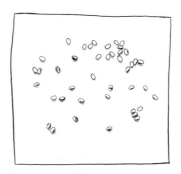

WHY I LOVE IT

I once received a wedding invitation on seed paper and it was such a beautiful touch – not only did I attend the wedding, but I also nurtured the blooms.

HOW YOU CAN USE THIS

Your seed paper can be made into notecards, writing paper or gift tags for friends. You could also make larger pieces of paper for gift wrap. Always include an instruction if you are giving this to someone, so the recipient will know how to look after the plants.

The seed paper should be kept totally dry until it is ready to be planted, as any contact with water will encourage the seeds to germinate. When you are ready to plant the seed paper, prepare a pot with soil. Place the seed paper under a thin layer of soil in a pot and water really well with warm water. Place the pot in sunny, warm spot like a window ledge and wait for the seeds to germinate.

MAKING IT YOUR OWN

With pressed flowers

Place pressed flowers onto the damp surface of your paper as it dries. The flatter the better for this, so go for buttercups, pansies, forget-me-nots or clovers.

With dried botanicals

For a little colour, add delicate dried botanicals (lavender, rose petals, calendula) into the paper mix along with the seeds or when you are mixing the pulp together.

By colouring the paper

You can also add colour to your paper, adding a powdered vegetable dye at the time of mixing. Beetroot powder will create a fuchsia pink, turmeric will give a vibrant yellow and spinach powder or wheatgrass powder will create green. Citrus zest adds a sprinkling of colour and fragrance. Simply grate it over the top and press down as you would with the seeds.

Why not try these mixes?

Chilli seeds, lime zest, rose petals
Wildflower seeds, blue cornflower petals, calendula petals
Basil seeds, ½ tsp green powdered colouring

Nature Printing on Fabric

· ·

This is where we really connect with the child within. We will start this craft with a walk while we gather some beautiful, interesting foliage to paint and stamp (I mean 'print'!) onto a piece of fabric. I do something like this with my own two girls but can get a little flustered over the squishing and squashing of petals and paint, lack of order and the 'give-up after 2 minutes' attitude. This grown-up version is an opportunity for us to take a slow and mindful approach to a kids' nature craft and create something beautiful in the process that can be turned into a cushion cover, a lampshade, a wall handing or accessory.

What you will need
Makes 1 printed fabric sheet

A selection of foliage: lavender, wheat, calendula, dandelion, ox-eye daisy, oak leaves, willow leaves

Acrylic paints

Paint palette/plate

Thick or flat paintbrush

A piece of fabric, cut to any size you like (I used white linen)

Baking parchment or brown paper

Method

Collect together some lovely, seasonal leaves, flowers and petals. Look for ones with waxy leaves with intricate veins, strong floral heads (like an ox-eye daisy) and recognizable silhouettes like wheat or lavender. The more detail and robust the flower or natural material the more successful the print will turn out – as I found out through a lot of trial and error.

Put your paint on a palette/plate and use your paintbrush to spread the paint out a little. Lay your fabric on a piece of baking parchment (the paint will go through to the other side when you press it on) or a mess-proof table covering. Now decide if you would like to create one big pattern using all of your materials at once (in which case follow Method A, below) or if you would like to do a repeated pattern (Method B).

Method A

To make a design using everything at once (like a collection), you need to take a stem or leaf and put it down into a thin layer of paint. Make sure it's coated on one side but not dripping in paint, then place it gently onto your fabric and leave it there. Do this with all of the materials until your fabric has all the items laid out onto it. Then get a large piece of parchment and cover it over the top. Carefully press down over each item with your hand or fingers and imprint all the painted details onto the fabric. When you have done each one, peel off the parchment, then individually peel off each natural item to reveal your nature prints.

Method B

To make a repeated design, lay your fabric flat on the parchment and then press an item into the thin layer of paint. Make sure it is coated on one side but not dripping in paint, then place it carefully onto the fabric. Put a piece of parchment on top and press over the item with your fingers. Take the parchment away and then lift off the flower or leaf to reveal your first print. Take the same flower or leaf again, wipe the paint off with parchment and repeat the steps in a symmetrical pattern. I use parchment here as you can wipe it clean and re-use it and the paint won't go through onto your work surface or fingers.

WHY I LOVE IT

I love this quiet, relaxed process of printing and making the most of the abundant materials found within nature. This activity offers a different type of art session for those who love to paint but feel they need a little creative encouragement.

MAKING IT YOUR OWN

Take a needle and thread and use a simple line stitch in a complementary colour to outline the printed flowers. Depending on your skill level of embroidery, you can really take this to the next level in terms of details and textures.

HOW YOU CAN USE THIS

When you have your printed fabric, wait for it to fully dry and then it can be used for many different art projects. For a simple homemade gift, you can trim your fabric to a suitable size and put it in a frame. You might also like to write the date and whatever flowers you've included on the back.

A Winter Picnic

. . . .

Picnics are a chance to turn your outdoor time with family or a loved one into a simple, magical occasion, but we don't have to wait for the warmer weather to embrace nature like this. With these few simple ideas, you can create a cosy picnic, a thoughtful celebration or add a joyful twist to your next wintry walk. I have included three different ways of embracing this kind of cool-weather picnic, so choose the one that suits you and feel free to adapt along the way!

For Romance

Whether it is Valentine's Day or a weeknight date, why not prepare a basket with romance in mind?

What you will need

A warm rug

Mittens/gloves

2 napkins rolled into enamel mugs

Jam jar with springs of holly or other foraged decoration

Tealight candle (electric) in lantern

Thermos of warm apple juice with slices of apple and cinnamon sticks to add

A couple of cheeses in parchment

A seasonal chutney or pickle

A pear, or small bunch grapes

A baguette or biscuits for cheese

Small platter to share

A knife

A travel-size game (Boggle, cards . . .)

For Families

Create a magical memory in the forest with this family-friendly picnic.
Sitting down at a halfway point on a walk is never a bad idea with children!

What you will need

A warm rug

Mittens/gloves

A small hot-water bottle

Nature reference book

Child-friendly mugs (i.e. ones that can't break)

Napkins rolled into enamel mugs

Thermos of hot chocolate (side of marshmallows)

Small jar of popcorn

Satsumas

Kilner jar of tomato soup

Baguette

Tealight candle (electric) in lantern

For Simple Joy

You might want to get outdoors but not have long to prepare, in which case a simple morning coffee and a comforting baked treat together under a tree will have to do!

What you will need

A warm rug

Mittens/gloves

Seat pads or easy-to-carry cushions

Napkins rolled into enamel mugs

Thermos of hot coffee

Side of milk

Pre-sliced banana loaf in parchment

WHY I LOVE IT

I love creating opportunities to embrace nature whatever the weather, and the potential for homemade touches is limitless. You can also really simplify this based on budget and time, so I hope that sharing this prompt and a few helpful hints will encourage you to try something similar.

HOW YOU CAN USE THIS

Picnics can be taken on the colder days through autumn and winter when you want to enhance your walk, or would rather opt for fresh air over restaurants or cinema trips.

MAKING IT YOUR OWN

Invite friends to join you and each bring one homemade item to literally make this activity your own.

Beach Trinket Tin

. . . .

Have you ever wondered what to do with all those shells? My family and I treasure shells found on seaside trips and look forward to planning beach-inspired art projects when home. Having gained a beautiful collection over the years, this project feels like the perfect way to honour them. A very kitsch, practical, nostalgic trinket tin made with shells and other natural materials, which you might find useful for pens, paintbrushes or dried flowers.

What you will need

Makes 1 tin

Rolling pin

500g block of air-dry clay (I use Das Clay)

Clean and dry tin can (sharp edge removed, see Tip on page 101)

Knife

Paintbrush

Water-like adhesive

Assortment of shells

Method

Roll out the clay until it is a rectangle, 25cm x 12.5cm. Roll the tin over the clay, taking the clay with you until it meets the end.

There will be a tiny crossover – if the crossover is too big, trim a bit off before fusing it. Turn the tin onto its bottom and tap it a few times to even the clay on the base. You can tidy the edge using the back of a knife to gently knock away the uneven bits (like pastry!). Then smooth the overlapping clay. Knock the top edge off or smooth it to round over the top of the tin.

Now, using a paintbrush and some water-like adhesive, arrange your shells onto the clay around the tin, making sure to press them down to hold. When the clay dries, they will secure.

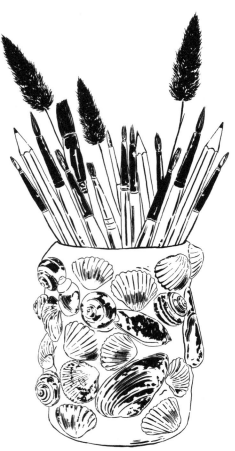

How to remove the sharp edge from a tin

Use pliers if you have them or a hammer if not and go all around the rim to ensure the sharp edge has been turned down and folded all the way into the tin.

WHY I LOVE IT

I made one of these and had it resting on a shelf to dry. A couple of ladies I work with commented on it and asked how I made it. It somehow looks much more complex than it is, but it also holds memory. It is nostalgic in its 'kitsch-ness' and in the way it takes you back, to that time, on that beach gathering shells.

HOW YOU CAN USE THIS

The tin can make a wonderful pen or brush pot, or, depending on whether you waterproof the inside of the tin, a plant/herb pot to be kept on the window ledge. It is eye-catching on a shelf just as it is, however, so it's perfect to simply keep any extra trinkets safe.

MAKING IT YOUR OWN

When I was making this shell pot, I was also eyeing up dried fruit, dried flowers and thinking about other things I could attach using the clay. I have lots of wooden letters in my kids' crafting box and thought I'd like to put a wooden letter in the centre of the tin, surrounded by the found treasures as a gift.

Dried Flower Hanging

· ·

We are going to bake our flowers for this craft. You can of course leave them out to air-dry over some weeks, but I wanted to show you another method of preserving flowers which means you can use them right away. It's a lovely way of savouring that bunch of flowers given for a special occasion or foraged by one of your children on a nature walk.

What you will need

Makes 1 hanging

Selection of flowers with stems

Baking tray

Baking parchment

Needle and thread

A large stick or branch

Bakers' string

Method

Take your stemmed flowers and lay them spaced out on a baking tray that's been lined with baking parchment. The blooms can stick a little, so the parchment will make them easier to lift off. Pop them into a cold oven and turn to the lowest setting – around 140°C/120°C Fan/gas mark 1 – and leave them for 2 hours, checking on them at the halfway point.

Once they are ready you will notice that they have shrunk somewhat. The colour will have also changed and certainly some will have kept their shape better than others. Trying a variety of flower stems is best to see what works for you. I had great success with blue cornflowers, baby's-breath, golden marguerite and lisianthus as well as rosemary and lavender.

Once you have your selection, push your needle and thread through the end of each stem, tying off to secure. You can cut the thread to a length of around 30cm or longer and varying lengths will look beautiful.

Space the dried flowers along your branch (the more gnarly and lichen-covered the better!), and tie them on with the loose end of the thread. When you lift your branch, you will have a curtain-like effect of dried flowers. To hang this, take a piece of bakers' string or twine and tie a long piece at each end of the branch.

WHY I LOVE IT

This is the more grown-up version of a hanging nature mobile, which is when you use a similar method to air-dry clay shapes, botanicals and feathers.

MAKING IT YOUR OWN

Adding aromatic herbs and lavender will make this botanical decoration even more appealing. Placing coloured ribbons between the stems or at the ends will add vibrancy.

HOW YOU CAN USE THIS

This can be hung up as a beautiful, natural decoration in your home, for a special occasion or to celebrate a season. Perhaps you have a bunch of flowers you are reluctant to part with and you want to preserve them in some way.

An Invitation . . .

To Celebrate

This was the first chapter I thought of when starting out with ideas for this book. I have loved homemade party decorations and crafting for celebrations for as long as I can remember. It has gone from being a necessity to save money and cut costs, to being a joyful process of connection and creative expression.

We currently have some bunting up in our kitchen that I made a few years ago from scraps of materials and twine with a handprinted 'H a p p y B i r t h d a y' spelled out on the triangles and a few feathers glued on. It was meant to be kept just for birthdays, but it has hardly been down. Three months after the last family birthday we had, and it is still strewn above the dining table in all its wonky, crafty charm.

I love to give a personal feel to a celebration and have always (where possible) tried to have a DIY attitude to parties. We had lots of handmade touches to our wedding day, too – I illustrated our invites and the church service sheets and hand-painted old wooden boards to use as sharing menus at the reception. Whether it is making gift bags for kids' parties, designing special celebration trails and altar-like birthday displays by candlelight, or Halloween's homemade, ghoulish games and chaotic, cornflour-filled piñatas, I get a lot from the making before the celebrating has even begun.

This chapter includes a versatile selection of crafting ideas that can add a little magic to a dinner table or gift or to adorn the home. Crepe Paper Flowers (see page 109), for example, can be placed in milk bottles for a different type of floral display, or even attached to DIY Party Crackers (see page 139). Fruit Fruit Decorations (page 114) have been used in homes since Victorian times and are far from losing their allure. I hope that, by the end, you will find you are inspired to add new learned skills and ideas into your next party preparation.

Quick Inspiration

· ·

CREATING A MOMENT

Celebration is a big word. It bursts with colour, fanfare, festival, glory and merriment. When I hear it, I immediately think of weddings, birthdays and festive holidays – a reason for a party and presents, for food, drink and music. However, 'celebration' also means observance and the act of honouring, and I want to prompt you here to look at other ways you can do this through the year, whether it is marking a new season or looking at a smaller occasion that deserves some reflection.

Before the summer holidays, I found myself crying on and off for seemingly no reason. I said to my husband, 'I feel grief, but I don't know why or where it's coming from,' all the while absentmindedly scrolling through the end-of-term emails about our eldest daughter, who would be leaving her nursery for pastures new – when to collect her bag of spare clothes, last pick-up times, plans for tea, cake and certificates. In my oblivion and lack of acceptance of her growing up, I hadn't thought to pause for her, or for myself, to honour the transition: all that has been achieved to this point and all the exciting adventures that lay ahead. In those last weeks of term I had been grieving the rush of time, waiting for the shock of the final nursery collection and the grateful, teary thank-yous. That last goodbye wave to her teacher. Leaving a nursery doesn't need a gala, but it does need 'a moment'.

If we look for opportunities in our lives to reflect on something special or sacred – be that just for ourselves, within the family or our group of friends – I am sure we might find a few that have been going unnoticed. It might be an equinox, solstice or full moon, the memory of a loved one passed or saying goodbye to a house or job.

Here are several ideas for how to create a different sort of celebration; one that is beautiful, simple and low-key.

Light a candle
You can light a candle to symbolize whatever you feel is right for you in that moment. This small act can bring comfort, give hope and offer light in the darkness.

Create an altar
Use candles, flowers, trinkets and photos to make a sacred space to mark an occasion. This could be for one event or it could be left up for a few weeks to honour a season or specific period in your life.

Create a nature mandala
Use natural materials to make a circular pattern on the ground. (I talk more about these on page 78.)

Discuss favourite moments with someone
Whether a simple phone call or in a group setting, reminiscing about past events encourages everyone involved to pause and reflect.

Make a gratitude list
Write a list of all the things you feel grateful for on the occasion or towards an event or person. Gratitude naturally slows us down and makes us feel positive.

Make a floating flower bowl

Add water to a large mixing bowl and carefully place some seasonal flower heads on the water, then display it in a prominent position.

Create a treasure hunt

This doesn't have to be for chocolates or gold but could be a chance to go on a little 'journey' and of course it provides lots of opportunity for simple joy and playfulness.

Have a fire

If you have a safe outdoor space to build a fire, then this is a great way to spend some time outdoors in the evening. Eat your meal, listen to music, chat or meditate in its warm glow. Sitting around a fire is my favourite way to celebrate, always.

Crepe Paper Flowers

. . . .

Making a crepe paper flower for the first time for this book, I was worried I was setting the bar too high for myself. I don't really have an 'intricate' touch, favouring clay, paint and twine, and so was worried that working with delicate paper might be for more highly skilled creatives. Of course, there is an incredible skill in making realistic paper flowers (and I highly recommend you look at the work of the Pom Pom Factory, Suzi McLaughlin or Tiffanie Turner – all exceptional resources for paper flowers and artistic floral design, see page 221) but today we will make our very own, beginner's-level paper flower, and I hope you will be as surprised in yourself as I was. In fact, my first single-stem purple crocus-like flower is in pride of place in my kitchen for all to see and brings a sense of pride and calm, as the making of this flower was truly meditative.

What you will need

Makes 1 crepe paper flower

For stem and leaf: 2 green crepe paper strips
(1.5cm x 25cm)

For pollen: 1 yellow crepe paper strip
(2.5cm x 12.5cm)

For petals: Any coloured crepe paper to cut
out 4 large petals, the size of your choice
(I find large, misshapen petals look best!)

Scissors

20cm piece of florists' wire

Glue stick

Pencil

Method

Prepare your crepe paper by cutting it into the sizes as above, then take your florists' wire and create a tiny hook at the top, pressing it down so it looks like the eye of needle.

Take a piece of your green paper and, starting at the hook end, wrap it diagonally down the wire until you reach the bottom. Glue the end to secure – your stem is done.

Take your yellow strip and, to create your pollen centre, fold it lengthways down the middle, then cut tiny little lines to this central point, all the way along one side of the strip, until you have a yellow fringe of paper. Now roll that fringed strip around the hook at the top of your wire and glue the end – it will look like a paper paintbrush!

For the petals, a teardrop shape is the best place to start as they are the easiest to attach. Use a pencil to draw them out gently onto the crepe paper; you want the ridges of the crepe paper to be vertical, as this makes the petal cut-outs more pliable.

One by one, attach the petals. To do so, use a dot of glue on the pointed part of the teardrop shape and stick it to the top the stem, then hold it down for 30 seconds before moving on to the next petal.

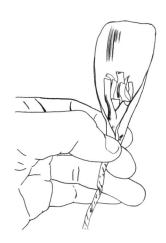

WHY I LOVE IT

Floral themes are always my favourite, and this makes a beautiful and delicate alternative to the real thing. This is a great starting point, but there is a whole world of paper floral design that is worth looking into further.

MAKING IT YOUR OWN

Have a go at making your own favourite flowers using the techniques and materials above – daisies, roses and lilies . . . You can also add watercolour paint onto the crepe paper for detail.

HOW YOU CAN USE THIS

Add your paper flowers to a table-scape, make as gifts for friends or put a single stem in a little glass bottle and keep it on a shelf in your home. Like the Dried Flower Hanging (see page 102), you could make several stems of flowers from paper and hang them in the same way to create a celebration garland.

Material Tie Garland

. . . .

I made one of these material garlands as a gift for friends celebrating Diwali, using amazing, hand-printed Indian fabric offcuts that I had left over from a craft project. I sat with tea and a biscuit and put it together one evening, and the process had a mindful feel to it. There's minimal mess involved, no stress, no sticking or stitching – just the repetition of tying of knots, which is incredibly relaxing once you get into a rhythm.

What you will need

Makes 1 garland

Fabric scissors

Bakers' string

Scraps of material (I cut about 50 strips around 20cm x 3cm in size for my large garland, but you can make them smaller)

Method

Cut your piece of string the length you would like your garland to be, then simply tie the fabric strips onto the string, one after the other. You can spread these out and have them hanging with space in between, or you can bunch them up.

When you have finished, you may like to tie a loop at either end of the string, so that you can easily hang the garland up when you are ready.

WHY I LOVE IT

A string of colourful material 'fireworks' to fill your home with celebration and joy – what is there not to love? It is simple and effective and the perfect project if you want a stress-free, last-minute homemade gift or decoration.

MAKING IT YOUR OWN

String other elements onto your garland between the fabric ties, such as pom-poms, beads and bells.

HOW YOU CAN USE THIS

As well as the hanging garland, you can also use this as a beautiful string to adorn a gift. Paired with brown paper, it doubles as gift-wrapping and can be given as a present in itself.

Dried Fruit Decorations

· ·

The aroma of baking oranges immediately transports me to festive times and the winter holiday season, and there is a cosy calm to these crafty preparations, which have now become a yearly ritual of mine. This is actually a very simple creative project which can be used with a variety of fruit for decorations and gifts or even cocktails or desserts. There is a knack to the width of the fruit slices and the way of baking them without burning them – trust me, I've burned many a batch! – so I hope this helps you to have great success with this very moreish and versatile creative prompt.

What you will need

Makes a selection of dried fruit decorations

Fruit, such as apples, oranges, lemons, limes, grapefruits

Chopping board

A sharp knife

Tea towel or kitchen roll

Wire baking rack or baking parchment on a baking tray

Optional: Craft varnish (I like Mod-podge)

For apples:

250ml water

½ tsp fine salt

Juice of 1 lemon

Mixing bowl

Method

The method for these decorations varies depending on which fruits you decide to use, apple or citrus fruits:

For Citrus Fruit

Cut each citrus fruit into slices of 1cm thickness (any thicker and you won't be able to dry them as easily). Lay your fruit slices out on your chopping board and using a tea towel or kitchen roll start pressing down and dabbing to absorb as much moisture from the slices as possible. Once you have done that, get your wire rack or your prepared tray and space out your fruit slices on it.

Put the tray or rack into the oven at 140°C/120°C Fan/gas mark 1. Your fruit will be slowly drying in here for around 2 hours. It is very easy for the fruit to burn and so I highly recommend checking at the 1-hour mark and turning everything over.

Once your fruit slices are dried, remove from the oven and leave to cool. If you would like to preserve the slices, you can cover them in craft varnish at this point.

For apples

Mix 250ml water, ½ teaspoon of fine salt and the juice of a lemon in a bowl. Allow the salt to dissolve. This solution will stop your apples from browning.

Get your chopping board and lay your apple on its side so the stem is horizontal. Cut round slices from the stem end as thinly as you like, remembering that the thinner they are, the quicker they will dry out. By cutting them this way, you will be left with a hole to thread string through if you want to hang them up later.

Soak your apple slices in the water for 5 minutes, then take them out and lay them flat on a piece of kitchen roll or a tea towel to dry off.

Once dry, spread your apple slices out onto the wire rack or prepared baking tray and put into the oven at 140°C/120°C Fan/gas mark 1. After an hour, check on them, turn them over, then put them back in for another hour. The apple slices will shrink slightly in size as they dry. Once they have dried out, remove from the oven and leave to cool. If you would like to preserve the slices, you can cover them in craft varnish at this point.

WHY I LOVE IT

I love using natural, easy-to-source materials in craft and decoration. For me this feels traditional; it reminds me of my own childhood making orange decorations with my sister or mum, and I hope my girls will do it too in many years to come.

HOW YOU CAN USE THIS

To make single fruit decorations

Get a piece of string about 15cm in length and thread it through the central hole of your fruit slice. Tie the thread at the top and create a loop to make a decoration.

To make a dried-fruit garland

Using a cocktail stick, make a little hole on one edge of each fruit slice and a second hole on the opposite edge. Using a stitch-like technique, thread your slices onto string so that your dried fruit will lay flat when you hang it up.

Napkin rings

Poke two holes into your dried fruit slices on opposite sides using a cocktail stick, as in the method for the garland (above). Get a piece of string about 15cm long and thread the string through the holes. Place a folded napkin on top and tie the string at the back.

Hurricane lanterns

Get a large glass vase and put a pillar candle in the middle. Ensure the candle is stable and on a flat surface. Place your dried fruit up to halfway up the candle. (Note: Make sure you always keep an eye on burning candles.)

Gift tags

Use the same method as a single fruit decoration (above), but get a little piece of brown paper or card, punch a hole in it, then thread this onto your string along with the fruit.

MAKING IT YOUR OWN

You can make this easy, natural decoration align with the seasons by simply thinking about what is available and growing locally to you at that time. If you are in the spring or summer months, then lemons and limes are ideal and perhaps a sprig of thyme, rosemary or lavender. The autumn is ideal for pears and apples and in winter, try quince and oranges, adding in cranberries and cloves to conjure incredible seasonal scents.

Winter Ice Lanterns

· ·

I set this up for my family last winter solstice. It was 5pm, and although it wasn't snowing – as it had been in the vision I'd had for the evening's celebrations – it was cold. Cold enough to make a little trail of ice lanterns that glistened and glowed in the growing darkness of the shortest day of the year.

What you will need

Makes 1 lantern

2 freezer-proof bowls of different sizes (if your freezer is full to the brim, then of course choose smaller bowls for your space)

A jug of water

Pebbles or other weighted items

Small tealight candles

Optional: Natural materials such as small pinecones, spruce, rosemary, cranberries; ice cubes

Method

Get your largest bowl and put any natural materials in the bottom, then rest your smaller bowl on top. The foliage will allow space under your second bowl for the water to fill around it, but if you haven't used any foliage then simply put a couple of ice cubes between the two bowls.

Place your weights (I use pebbles) into your smaller bowl – this will stop the bowl moving.

Now you can pour your water into the large bowl, so it fills the space between to the two bowls. Fill this to just below the top of the bowl, to prevent spillages when transferring over to the freezer. Put your bowl in the freezer and leave for 12 hours.

When you bring the bowls out, check the water is completely frozen by pressing your finger onto the ice. If you are confident it has frozen all the way through, remove your weights, then the bowl, and tip the larger bowl over onto a tray. If you struggle to remove your bowls at all, running a little warm water over the top will loosen them.

Turn your ice bowl the rightway up again, place your tealight candles in the centre, and light!

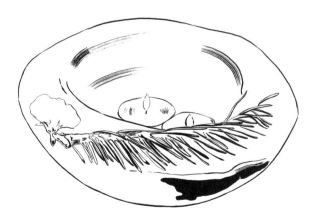

WHY I LOVE IT

These ice lanterns create a sort of magic . . . maybe it is the enchantment, the glow or the cosiness of a flicker of warm light on a cold evening. They are such a special thing to introduce to your time outdoors, enjoying nature and celebration.

MAKING IT YOUR OWN

Use this exact same method to make an ice bowl for a summer party, fill with strawberries or ice cream, and swap the winter foliage for rose petals, daisies or sliced citrus fruit.

HOW YOU CAN USE THIS

You can apply this same method to cylindrical shapes, tins and Bundt cake tins, which don't need a second bowl as they can be flipped over and the candle placed in the hole in the middle. Play around with the many ways you can fill and present your ice lanterns. Lay them out on a cold evening or put them on a saucer on your front doorstep if it's safe to do so.

A Wreath (For Any Occasion)

· ·

A wreath is a circle of foliage used as a symbol of honour, celebration and joy. You may have seen a dried wreath of barley around harvest time, or evergreen wreaths hanging on doors during the winter. In Ancient Greek and Roman times, wreaths were worn around the head to denote status or victory, and to this day can be seen in our modern Olympic ceremonies. For me, the wreath invites us into a season, showcasing what nature has to offer and reminding us to stay connected to the time of year. Wreaths are also beautiful to look at and bring life to any occasion.

The living wreath is a wonderful way of welcoming the awakening of nature around Easter and through spring. The cool temperatures aren't so harsh that they will harm the blooms but it's also not so warm as to scorch it all. A living wreath is exactly what it sounds like: it is alive, and in attaching your bulbs with soil and damp moss and careful binding, you will be able to watch as your sweet flowers start to appear over the following weeks. It is a true wonder to watch as this wreath blossoms before your eyes.

An aromatic wreath is perfect for the summer months. It will only get better as it dries out and the scent enhanced by the sunny, summer days: rosemary and lavender whirling around with the dried lemon. In warm weather, you want to choose foliage that will not need maintenance with water. This is meant to bring joy, after all, not become a full-time job!

Festive wreaths are the type we are probably all most familiar with, and I've kept this one very traditional. Known winter smells like eucalyptus, fir and oranges will be a warm welcome to anyone visiting for Christmas or winter celebrations.

What you will need

Makes 1 wreath

1 natural wreath ring (I use one that is 30cm in diameter, but please choose a size that suits you)

Sheets of living moss (see note on page 124)

Florists' wire or transparent thread

Scissors

Twine/ribbon/fabric (this is to hang, wrap around or add bow features)

For a living wreath
3 hyacinth bulbs (they are going to flower on the wreath)

3 narcissus bulbs (they can be just flowering or flowered)

4 sprigs of foliage like willow, pussy willow, eucalyptus or clematis

For an aromatic wreath
10 stems of lavender (freshly cut or dried)

A small bunch of chamomile flowers

4 sprigs of rosemary

4 sprigs of thyme

2 sprigs of bay

Dried lemon or grapefruit slices (see page 114)

For a festive wreath

4 sprigs of eucalyptus

10 or more sprigs of pine or fir

3–6 pinecones

Dried orange slices (see page 114)

Which moss should I use?

You can add moss to your wreath for coverage of thread/string but it also creates a beautiful, organic and earthy bed for your decorations. You might be able to get sheet moss/living moss at your local garden centre or florist. Alternatively, have a look online. If you are foraging moss, please only take a small amount as it is a very important part of the forest/woodland ecosystem.

Method

We are going to start all our wreaths the same way, so whatever wreath you have chosen to make, we will all be working with the same 'canvas'. First, wrap the sheets of moss around your natural wreath ring, either sporadically or all the way around to cover it completely. The moss provides a lovely lush green base for the wreath, and for the living wreath provides necessary moisture for your bulbs.

Get your florists' wire or transparent thread and wrap it around your ring once and tie. Then, without cutting it, start to go over the moss sheets (not too tight; just secure enough to hold), coming back to the middle and working around in one direction. When you are happy with the coverage, you can either leave your wire attached and use this as your starting point to add extra materials, or you can tie it at the back of the ring and cut it away. I like to do a mock-up to work out where to place things, so I don't secure anything at this stage; I just lay my materials on top of the ring. This way, I know how much to use and where to begin.

For a living wreath
To make your living wreath, take the hyacinth and narcissus bulbs and position them on the wreath. Get a little bit of moss and use a water spray to spritz it all over; it should be damp but not dripping. You are then going to use this like a blanket to secure over the bulb. Using your florists' wire, go around this moss blanket and tie at the back of the ring, then wrap it around to secure the bulb – but, again, not too tightly, as you do not want to strangle the bulb. Finally, position your sprigs of foliage around your wreath and secure them with a little wire.

For an aromatic wreath
To make the aromatic wreath, depending on the size of the foliage, you can either bunch it together in a posy and tie up with twine or ribbon, then attach to the ring over the moss with florists' wire, or you can attach each sprig near to the end of the branch or stalk onto the moss using florists' wire, then place another one slightly lower down over the top, attach and repeat until your sprigs cover the ring all around (this is a great technique when using fir or pine on the festive wreath).

For a festive wreath
For the festive wreath, attach the foliage as described in the aromatic wreath method above. To attach single stems, pinecones and citrus fruits, you can use a hairpin method. For this, cut off a bit of florists' wire

about 10cm long for small items, 15cm for larger items. Bend it in half so it looks like a hair pin, then hold your item onto the ring and slide the 'hairpin' through the item and the moss on an angle to secure.

To finish your wreath you will need a minimum 30cm length of twine, ribbon or fabric. Tie it securely around the very central, top part of the wreath, and with the remaining ends create a loop and double tie it off, so that you can hang the wreath up over a door handle, gate post or wherever you wish to present it. You can also leave the ends loose to tie it directly into position.

WHY I LOVE IT

A wreath brings so much joy hung on the front door, whether it is the scent that emerges, the buds, or the pure celebration of the season. It will always provide a warm welcome. Once you have mastered a few basic techniques, you can work with such a variety of different materials, too, from dried flowers to small decorations and trinkets.

HOW YOU CAN USE THIS

Hang your wreath on your front gate or door. Lay it flat as a table centrepiece, perhaps with a cheese board or pillar candle inside, or give one as a gift.

MAKING IT YOUR OWN

Use my notes above as guidance, but explore other seasonal varieties. Try out coloured ribbons or wrap fabric offcuts around the ring instead of moss. You could also use this method to create a wreath head-dress. You will be able to source natural wreath rings of all sizes, so choose the right fit for you and add some soft moss or fabric underneath so it sits comfortably on your head.

Painted Glass Carafes

· ·

I have been ogling painted glass carafes on Instagram and Pinterest for a while, longing to create my own glassware range with floral designs and folksy symbols. There is romance to painted glass, reminding me of treasures seen in museums, intricate scenes painted onto apothecary bottles. I love the storytelling aspect of an art project and with something like this you can really embrace that. I will guide you with a few brush techniques too, so that you can explore your own style and create something totally unique.

What you will need
Makes 1 painted glass carafe

Paper

Pen

A water carafe or smooth, glass vase or jar

Tea towel

Paint palette/plate

Glass paint (see Note on page 130)

1 or more round, pointed-tip paintbrushes

Small bowl of water

Kitchen roll

Method

Before starting, prepare your space. Having tools and materials ready is half the effort, so once you have it all laid out, you are ready to go. Also, make sure you're sitting comfortably, as you might be in the same position for a while as you paint.

Using your paper and pen, you can put together your design or practise if you haven't done anything artistic in a while. Keep it simple at first, and once you are in your flow, you will work out where you want to go with it. When you are painting onto your carafe, don't forget you can wipe it off before it dries, so don't panic about doing anything wrong and feel free to play around with it.

If you don't know where to start with your design, I recommend going to page 24 and using the exercise here to ignite your creativity.

Wipe your glass with your tea towel to make sure it is completely clean and dry, then pour your chosen paint colours (only a little at a time) onto your palette or plate. Dab your pointed paintbrush into your water first briefly and then into your chosen colour, coating the tip of the brush in the paint.

I have found that with glass paints, the best way of applying them is in dots, dabs and brief strokes rather than continuous paint strokes, as the paint has a rather sticky and thick consistency. If you are using acrylics, this will be much more smooth and flowing, and you'll need only a little water to get you started.

If you want to layer your colours, start with the lighter colours, wait for them to dry and then apply the darker tones on top. Use the same method if you want a more opaque effect – paint one coat, wait for it to dry, then put the second coat on.

Once you have completed your glass painting, leave to dry for 24 hours before using and make sure to wash your brushes thoroughly.

Which glass paint should I use?

You can buy glass paint from most craft stores and it will stay on when hand-washed gently. If you do not have glass paint, you can use acrylics for a temporary effect, perfect for a table setting, but be aware that it will wash off.

WHY I LOVE IT

I like painting, be that on garden sheds or canvas, but there is something particularly satisfying about painting on glass, and although it feels quite 'expert', it is actually something that anyone can enjoy.

HOW YOU CAN USE THIS

Using a small glass jar, you can paint on a name and use as a place setting with a couple of floral sprigs. Alternatively, it would make the perfect personalized toothbrush holder for family members, or fancy, decorative treat jars. I use mine as a pen jar and have one on my bedside table with water in.

MAKING IT YOUR OWN

Create a design based on something that is meaningful for you. If this is for a birthday celebration, perhaps choose to paint the flower of that month, or if it's a gift for a friend, maybe select three things that remind you of them and paint them in – it could be anything from a shell to a paw print, a heart or a daisy. Use a repeated pattern or add a border or lines of dots.

Glass carafe design ideas

FLOWERS

DOTS

SINGLE SWEEP
BRUSHSTROKES

ROSES WITH
SINGLE BRUSHSTROKES

Punched Hole Lanterns

. . . .

These are rustic, upcycled lanterns of joy, and I absolutely love the magical effect they have as they illuminate the room with their glowing patterns. The hammering technique is also really cathartic, even with the simplest design.

Note: The lanterns get very hot when using real candles, so I suggest using electric tealights for this craft. If you are using a real tealight candle, put your tin lantern onto a saucer for safety when moving it and don't leave unattended.

What you will need

Makes 1 lantern

A food tin (sharp edge removed; see Tip on page 101)

Chopping board

Tea towel

1 nail

Hammer

Electric tealight (or a real candle)

Optional: Sharpie pen or paper with tape

Method

Fill your tin with water and pop it into the freezer for a couple of hours until it has completely frozen. The ice block inside will enable you to hammer around the tin easily when punching in your decorative holes. Set up a chopping board with a tea towel folded on top – this will secure the tin and also catch any melting water.

You can either draw a design onto a piece of paper and tape it around the tin, or you can you use a pen to mark out the design (Sharpies work best). I have included a few design ideas on page 135 to give you a prompt for some designs that are really effective.

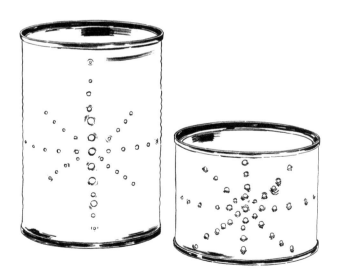

Now for the fun bit! Take your nail and place it over part of the design and hammer a couple of times until you create a small hole. Then go around the design and use this method to create spaced-out dots along your design.

When you have finished your design, tip the ice block out. If the bottom of your tin has bowed (this can happen when it's in the freezer), then hammer it back down again, so that the tin will stand flat. Pop an electric tealight candle into the tin and, voila, you have yourself a homemade punched hole lantern!

WHY I LOVE IT

This is a particularly brilliant camping activity. If you don't have access to a freezer, then you can use small stones (or pebbles from the beach!) instead. When you switch the tealights on, or light the candle, the punched hole design reflects such a beautiful pattern across the space you're in, instantly adding magic to any environment.

HOW YOU CAN USE THIS

These can be used as lanterns for a table scape, kitchen utensil or pencil/paintbrush holders, or even hung in trees (electric tealights only).

MAKING IT YOUR OWN

You can paint the tin after you have punched the holes in, using acrylic paint – or sample pots of wall paint work well, too! This means you can really personalize these for any themed party, indoor or out. You can also add little handles, which make them perfect for hanging around trees with electric or solar lights.

Lantern hole punching design ideas

Colourful Tassles

· ·

This quick craft can be adapted easily and used to bring vibrancy, colour and fun to clothing, gifts and decorations. Very simple to make once you know how and a beautiful finishing touch for your creative projects, these colourful tassels work really well as an addition to many of the crafts in this book.

What you will need

Makes 1 tassel

Scissors

1 piece of cardboard

3 reels of wool in different colours

Method

Cut a piece of cardboard to the length you would like the tassel. Cut 3 pieces of wool the length you would like the loop at the top, using three different colours. Get a reel of wool and start to wind it lengthways around the cardboard. You want to wrap it around so that the wool becomes thick, like a tassel.

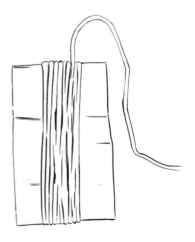

Now, take the three long pieces of cut wool for the loop, thread them through the top end of the wrapped wool and tie tightly to secure, leaving the long ends hanging. Snip the wool along the bottom edge of the cardboard to release the strands of wool.

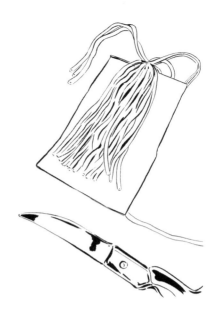

Take another small piece of wool and, about two fingers' width from the top, tie the wool tightly around the wrapped wool, then cut the ends off. It should now look like a tassel. To finish, tie together the three pieces of wool to make a loop. I also like to plait the three strands of wool for a different design.

WHY I LOVE IT

This craft is quick and easy to learn and encourages a quiet connectedness during the winding, looping and use of hands.

MAKING IT YOUR OWN

Why not make a few, then thread them onto a piece of string, putting an air-dried clay bead in between each one. A beautiful DIY garland for your home or celebration!

HOW YOU CAN USE THIS

Tassels make beautiful gift tag decorations, napkin rings, key rings or bag accessories and are great additions to knitting projects too. I also discovered they make a great toy for kittens!

DIY Party Crackers

· ·

If lockdown taught us anything, it's how to get crafty with a toilet roll! These don't have the snap and bang of a standard Christmas cracker (I did think about it . . .) but this is an easy and sweet idea for a table setting, party favour or even to give as a gift, and as always, we are trying to use things we might have at home already. As with the Crepe Paper Flowers (see page 109), I have used crepe paper for these crackers, having found tissue paper too delicate, but you can also use material like cotton or linen in the same way.

What you will need
Makes 1 cracker

Toilet-roll tube (or a kitchen-roll tube cut in half)

A piece of crepe paper, wrapping paper or brown Kraft paper

Scissors

A small treat or gift to put inside

Glue stick

2 pieces of twine, ribbon or material strips

Optional: A magazine for cut-out images

Method

Pop your toilet-roll tube onto the crepe paper and cut the paper so that it leaves 10–12cm of paper at each end of the cracker (if it's any less, it will be too short when you gather it to tie).

Nestle your treat or gift into the middle of the tube and then wrap the paper around it. If you are using crepe paper then it holds really well if you gather and twist it, otherwise you might like to put a dot of glue onto the middle of the paper to help it hold while you tie the ends. Now get your pieces of ribbon or string and tie the paper very tightly at each end – an instant cracker!

For a kitsch touch, cut out a selection of fun or themed pictures from a magazine, then choose one image per cracker, dot glue onto the picture and place on the middle of the tubed area.

WHY I LOVE IT

These small, sweet and surprising crackers are easy to make and immediately bring an extra-special element to an occasion. You can take the customization in any direction you like, which makes this a really fun and playful craft for any skill level.

HOW YOU CAN USE THIS

As well using as gifts and party favours, another idea would be to create a fun dinner-party game. Include notes of paper with clues in each cracker for an easy 'treasure' hunt, a murder mystery or game of charades.

MAKING IT YOUR OWN

You can add Crepe Paper Flowers (page 109), Salt-Dough Tags (see page 171) or dried flowers (see page 102) tied onto one end to jazz up your crackers. If you have beautiful writing (I do not!) then perhaps use a chalk pen to write across the cracker, or you could add hand-painted flowers with some acrylics.

An Invitation . . .

To Give

Being generous is good for the soul . . . whether that is the feel-good warmth of gifting to a friend or giving your time to help someone in need, it has been proven that generosity impacts us enormously. More specifically, being 'of service' reduces our stress levels, increases feelings of happiness,[9] and enhances our life's purpose.

There is no question that when I start to feel flat and a little joyless, if I take a look at my life in that moment I often find am not doing enough for other people. I don't mean as a mother (I am always doing a lot within the family); I am talking about going out of my way, changing my path, or stopping to think: What can I do to bring someone else joy? What can I do to help? What can I give? The more effort I make to be kind to others (especially when they don't expect it), the happier and more enthused I am overall, and so I wasn't surprised to learn that kindness boosts our oxytocin, dopamine and serotonin levels as well as creating that wonderful domino effect of positivity in those around us.

My hope for this chapter is that you will feel confident in creating opportunities to give from the heart with simple, homespun offerings and prompts. Making things from scratch is something we are seeing a lot more of, as people work from home a lot more, while trying to be eco-friendly and frugal. Even if saving money on buying gifts is the entry point for enjoying all things homemade, the creative exercise in itself offers us so much for our well-being, and we can find ourselves embracing the making, experimentation and the re-connection with play as a result.

So, as you approach this chapter, I invite you to be open to kindness, to giving and to being confident in your homemade capabilities, whatever your level of skill, because that honest and heartfelt intention will emanate from whatever the gift is that you are passing on.

Quick Inspiration

. . . .

HOMEMADE CARDS AND LETTER WRITING

I make most of the cards I send for birthdays, thankyous and Christmas, and at times a bit of last-minute creativity has been essential for a forgotten birthday, breezing in to save the day!

Homemade cards and letters are fantastic for so many reasons. They are both so personal and you can tailor a card's design to the person you are writing to. It will prompt you to slow down for a moment and reflect on the recipient. The receiver will love the thought and creativity that goes into it and even if you don't consider yourself someone who is 'arts and crafty', it is still possible to make something meaningful.

My best friend Lara sends beautiful correspondence, whether it's a thankyou or just a 'thinking of you' note. I see her elaborate writing on an envelope when the post arrives and I always feel comforted. She says of sending notes and letters: 'You can be a little more earnest. It's hard to be earnest in day-to-day interactions. You can say things you might not really want to say in person. They are charming to send and receive' – and this is true. How often have we seen someone or been in a group and then afterwards thought I wish I'd told them . . . ? Of course we have texts, WhatsApp, emails, social media and phone calls, but putting pen to paper does seem to make our thoughts flow differently. Like journalling, there is a catharsis, a kind of therapy in letting the words trickle out.

Here are some good and encouraging starting points if you want to find your own love of homemade cards and letter writing . . .

✳ Add a pack of plain envelopes to your stationery collection.

✳ Buy stamps and keep them to hand. If you have stamps, you will be much more inclined to send post.

✳ Keep a good pen that you enjoy writing with – I have recently rediscovered fountain pens!

✳ Have a box of scrap paper and offcuts of wrapping paper, which you can repurpose to collage onto your cards.

✳ Be inspired by the person you are sending to – what do they enjoy? What is the occasion? Make it personal, whether in art form or in your writing.

✳ Date your cards or letter; it is a lovely moment for the receiver.

✳ When in doubt, send a postcard!

And finally . . . if it occurs to you to reach out to someone by mail and you think it will bring them cheer, then you should absolutely do it!

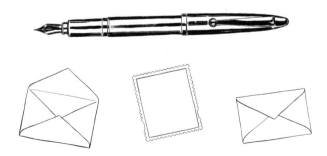

Soap on a Rope

· ·

I went into a little rabbit hole when researching soap making. There are so many beautiful, natural, interesting ways of making soaps, and once you start looking, you can see how it would be easy to change your whole beauty and housekeeping routine by simply shifting products to multi-use, eco-friendly soap variations – shampoo bars for your hair, exfoliating bars for your body, dish-soap bars on string to hang on your taps . . . This is an entry-level activity, however, and that is because instead of trying to fumble my way through a cold-pressed, from scratch, organic tutorial of which I know very little about (but am

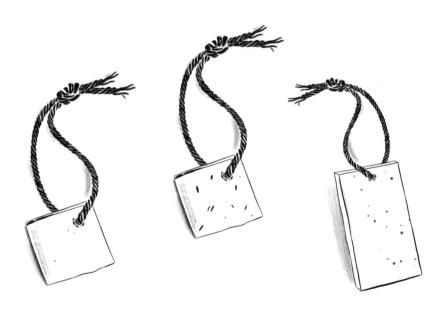

keen to learn!), I decided to introduce you to something that is easy to get hold of, easy to use and safe for beginners to explore with little or no experience . . . and that is 'melt and pour'.

'Melt and pour soap' is the name for a large block of pre-mixed soap base, meaning the chemistry part has already been done for you. Look for organic soap bases and explore the different types you can buy, like goat's milk, oat, white or clear, then have some fun with it! Here I'll show you how to make a honey, sweet orange and poppy seed layered soap on a rope.

What you will need

Makes 10 small soaps

A block of white 'melt and pour' soap (1kg)

2 large heatproof mixing bowls

Saucepan

Silicone spatula/metal spoon

Kitchen roll

Silicone loaf tin (see Tip on page 149)

Witch hazel or vodka in a small spray bottle

1 tbsp poppy seeds

1½ tbsp honey

10 drops sweet orange essential oil

Chopping board

Sharp knife

Skewer

Bakers' or waxed string

Baking parchment

Method

Chop your 'melt and pour' block up into smaller cubes and put them in a heatproof bowl. Place the bowl over a saucepan of water on the stove and heat until the soap blocks have melted. Make sure the base of the bowl isn't touching the hot water. You may need to stir a few times as a skin develops on top during the process which requires it to be folded in. Put your spatula or metal spoon onto a piece of kitchen roll so it doesn't make a mess of your surface.

Take your silicone loaf tray and put it to the side of your soap-melting station. Get your small spray bottle of witch hazel or vodka ready – this will be used to spray over the soap surface once it has been poured to get rid of air bubbles.

Which moulds should I use?

A silicone cupcake tray will also work really well. Whatever you are using, you want something heatproof that you will be able to easily remove your soap from.

Once your soap has melted, turn your cooker off and carefully lift your bowl to the side (be careful of the steam which will come from your pan). Keep the pan of water, as we will use it again. Now you will need to split your melted soap, so take your second heatproof bowl and transfer 10 tablespoons of melted soap into it before putting it aside.

To your larger quantity of soap, add the poppy seeds and stir through until well distributed. Pour the mixture into the silicone loaf tray and spray a little witch hazel or vodka over the surface to get rid of air bubbles. Leave to solidify for 30 minutes.

After 20 minutes has gone by, put your second bowl back onto the bain-marie and re-melt the soap base. When it has completely melted, add the honey and sweet orange essential oil and stir thoroughly. The soap will turn a lovely golden colour.

Your poppy seed soap should be solid now, but touch it gently with your finger to check. If it is, then you are ready to pour the second batch of soap on top. Make sure the golden soap covers the whole surface, so move around when you're pouring.

After leaving to set for 1 hour, gently press your soap along the top and through the side of the tin. When you are satisfied that it is completely solid, you can pop the block out of the mould onto a chopping board then, satisfyingly, cut your slices like a loaf of bread until you have ten perfect, layered soaps.

To put rope through these, wiggle the skewer gently through a corner of the poppy seed layer until you have a lovely, rounded hole (don't skewer through the honey layer as it will be too thin and might split). Cut your string to 20cm and twist the end, then poke it through the hole and tie.

Note: If you are pregnant, please only use essential oils if you have checked their suitability.

WHY I LOVE IT

This may be entry level soap making, but the feeling of achievement when you are looking at your bars of soap or your soap on a rope is really something. I also challenge you not to find cutting through the soap incredibly moreish!

HOW YOU CAN USE THIS

This is the perfect soap to hang from the tap or in the shower and won't leave a mark or get stuck to a shelf. It also makes a wonderful and thoughtful gift Either wrap individually in baking parchment or stack them in a pair and seal with a brown Kraft label.

MAKING IT YOUR OWN

Explore natural colourings and mineral powders that are good for the skin, or add skin-friendly exfoliating components like oats or Himalayan salt. If you want to feature a word on the soap, then just before it hardens press alphabet wooden stampers onto the face of the soap – perfect if you are making 'dish soap' or customized soap as a gift.

Jam-Jar Candle

· ·

Candle making invokes the same heart-warming, comforting and calming peace of mind that can be found in the atmosphere of sitting with the flickering, glowing light. The rhythm and feel of being huddled over the stove, melting the batches of wax, then setting up the jars and pairing scents feels traditional, slow and present. It is a great craft to do with a circle of like-minded, time-honouring friends, or as a different kind of soul care.

This method is really simple and, like some of the other crafts you will find in this book, my hope is that by including a beginner's-style, back-to-basics recipe for luxury items (just like with the soap recipe on page 146), you will feel inspired to go on and learn more, discovering the many incredible people doing it in more advanced ways.

I like using soy wax because it burns for longer and is easier to clean up afterwards. When it comes to sourcing jars or containers, I use Mason jars, but you can use whatever you have at home – just make sure that they are heatproof and appropriate for candles! For this method, we are using the jar you choose to measure out your pellets, which is why there are no quantities in the recipe, as it will be different for everyone.

What you will need

Makes 1 jam jar candle

1 jar/container of your choice

Cotton candle wick(s)

Kitchen roll or tray

Heatproof mixing bowl

Saucepan

Soy wax pellets

Clothes peg

Essential oil of your choice (see Tip below)

Heatproof pouring jug

Tea towel or oven mitts

Scissors

How to use essential oils

Essential oils have incredible healing properties and their scent is powerful, but when used in candle-making, you need a large amount to provide a noticeable aroma. If bought from a good distributor, essential oils are the pure and natural option, but you can also look at 'fragrance oils', which are cheaper to use. You can find 'fragrance calculators' online which do the hard part for you when it comes to quantities, but generally for every 100g of wax, you will need to use between 8 and 10 grams of essential oil. I recommend measuring it out using scales. If you are pregnant, please only use essential oils if you have checked their suitability.

Method

First, clean your jar and dry it thoroughly, then set it out with the candle wick on a piece of kitchen roll or a tray to catch any drips. If you are making more than one candle, set everything out now. Set up your bain-marie by bringing a saucepan of water to a boil and putting a heatproof bowl on top of it. Make sure the base of the bowl doesn't touch the hot water.

Now measure your wax by filling your jar 2.5 times with wax pellets. Put them into the bowl over the boiling water and slowly allow the wax to melt; there is no need to stir. Meanwhile, get your candle wick (or wicks if you'd like more than one!), dip the end with the metal tab into the melting wax and then immediately place it into the centre of your jar to set and hold. Now clip your clothes peg so that it secures the wick in place, balancing it over the lip of the jar. This will help keep the wick steady when you come to pouring the wax in.

After 10 minutes, your wax pellets should be melted. If there are a few pellets left, just leave it an extra minute or so, then add your essential oil.

Very carefully decant your wax into a heatproof jug; I use a measuring jug. (The bowl will be hot so use a tea towel or oven mitts.) Pour the wax into your jar and stop just before the line where you might twist on a lid, or about 2cm from the top. Leave your candle to set for 24 hours somewhere cool and then take off the peg. Cut the wick so that there is about 0.5cm above the surface of the candle.

HOW YOU CAN USE THIS

Add this to your own self-care routine, or make one with citronella essential oil and put it in a plant pot or heatproof bowl to keep mosquitoes away on summer nights outdoors. Pop the lid on then tie a little jute ribbon around the middle with a dried stem of lavender woven through, or tie string around the top to add your gift tag. (Note: Remind friends to remove the string and card before lighting!)

WHY I LOVE IT

I was put off candle making for a long time because I thought it might be too scientific for me. However, once I had tried a simplified method and played around with quantities of scent, containers and wax, I got hooked immediately and went on a batch candle-making session over the festive period, conjuring Christmas aromas in the kitchen. Presents were made very easy that year!

MAKING IT YOUR OWN

Why not add the method found on page 127 for painting glass carafes and paint your jar first, before filling with wax and giving someone the most perfect, customized homemade gift!

Whipped Body Butter

· ·

The word 'butter' immediately makes me think 'silky . . . luxurious . . . indulgent . . . spreadable', so when I discovered how easy and effective it was to make my own whipped version to nourish my skin, I was ready to lather myself in it. Not only does it provide deep moisture to dry or chapped skin, it also smells and looks good enough to eat. Keep it in the fridge, taking it out a few minutes before you plan to use it.

What you will need

Makes 1 x 500ml jar of butter

Saucepan

Heatproof mixing bowl

1 cup shea or cocoa butter (raw, unrefined, will mostly come solid)

¼ cup oil (I like coconut oil, jojoba oil or sweet almond oil)

10 drops essential oil

Electric whisk

Silicone spatula

Jam jar with lid (sterilized and dry)

Optional: 2 drops rosehip or vitamin E oil for very dry skin

Method

Set up your bain-marie by bringing a saucepan of water to a boil and putting a heatproof bowl on top of it. Make sure the base of the bowl doesn't touch the hot water.

Add the shea butter (or cocoa butter) to the bowl and allow to melt. Then add ¼ cup of oil. Mix, cover and put into the freezer for 20 minutes. The mixture will be ready when you can put your finger onto it and it leaves a dent. If it is too hard, then re-melt and try this part again.

Once out of the cooling phase, add your essential oil and any additional nourishing oil and whisk with an electric whisk for 5 minutes or until it forms soft peaks. Use your spatula to bring it in from the edges of the bowl.

You should end up with a mixture the consistency of whipped butter and you can now spoon this into your jar. Label and store in a cool dark place or the fridge until you are ready to use. (The mixture will liquify if left in a warm place.) If stored correctly, it will keep for 3 months.

Note: If you are pregnant, please only use essential oils if you have checked their suitability.

WHY I LOVE IT

I never thought I'd be able to make a cream for my skin that had the appearance and feel of a high-end, expensive, store-bought product – until I made this! It's incredible, low-cost and fun to make.

MAKING IT YOUR OWN

Using cocoa butter and adding a few drops of orange essential oil will create the exact scent of a 'chocolate orange', so play around with scents and oils and make equally delicious discoveries.

HOW YOU CAN USE THIS

A homemade potion is a luxurious gift idea for a loved one and your friends won't believe you made this. Package it up in a beautiful jar and remember to label with all ingredients and the date it was created.

Furoshiki Gift Wrapping

As many of us make more sustainable decisions in our homes and in relation to our consumerism, we are in turn connecting more with tradition, with craft and with our own creativity as we think of new ways to cook meals, DIY and give gifts. When I first spotted a present in furoshiki wrapping cloth, I immediately wanted to learn how to do it myself and find out how this tradition started, because it made sense to me from a practical point of view that you would give a gift that can be kept and appreciated in its entirety, with nothing going to waste!

Furoshiki means 'bath spread' in Japanese, and these traditional wrapping cloths were originally used as far back as the seventeenth century to wrap and bundle clothes when going to the bathhouses.[10]

The cloths were mostly square and were made from fabrics like cotton and silk, featuring beautiful and intricate designs, patterns and pictures.

What you will need

Makes 1 furoshiki-wrapped present

A piece of fabric, 50cm x 50cm (see Tip on page 160)

A stem of rosemary, eucalyptus or dried wheat

A gift

Method

Place your fabric square on a flat surface so that it resembles a diamond. The bottom corner should be pointing towards you.

Place your gift in the centre of the fabric and fold the bottom corner over the top of the gift. Reach over and bring the top corner towards you and tuck the excess corner of fabric under the gift.

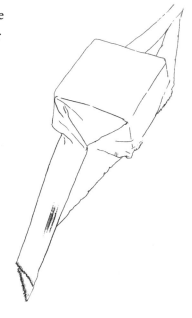

Now go to the left corner of fabric, fold it in slightly nearest to the gift like you would when wrapping the end of a present with paper (see illustration, right), and then bring it over the gift. Do the same on the other corner.

Now you have both your 'handles' ready to tie in the middle with a secure bow or knot. Place your botanical stem through the middle, and it's ready to send!

What size fabric?

I have included a large and useful measurement that will fit a variety of gift sizes, but generally you want the fabric to be three times the size of your gift so it goes all the way around. It is better if there is more fabric as you can just tuck it under.

WHY I LOVE IT

This is an eco-friendly choice when thinking about how to wrap or bundle up a gift – I would recommend looking in your local charity shop for any vintage or pre-loved pocket squares or handkerchiefs.

HOW YOU CAN USE THIS

As well as wrapping a gift, you could also bundle a loaf of bread and leave it as a little token for a neighbour or relative.

MAKING IT YOUR OWN

If you want to get really creative here, then cut a piece of natural cotton canvas fabric to size and paint your own design onto the fabric using acrylic paints. Leave to dry fully before putting it to great use!

Clay Diffuser Beads

· ·

I did this by chance when trying to make some clay beads for my daughter to thread onto a necklace. Once they had dried, I decided to experiment with dropping on some essential oil (necklace immediately put on the back burner!) and I noticed how well the porous clay held the aroma. I had my faithful bag of fabric scraps and I came up with ideas for the craft that follows!

What you will need
Makes several bead diffusers

500g block of air-dry clay (I use Das Clay)

Baking tray

Paintbrush or cocktail stick

Fabric cut into strips of 20cm x 1.5cm

Essential oil of your choice

Method
Break off enough clay to roll into a ball around the size of a conker. The ball should be smooth with no cracks (if you do have any cracks, then use a tiny drop of water to smooth it over). If you are happy with this size, then repeat with your remaining clay until you have all the balls, then spread them out on a baking tray.

Get your paintbrush (use the handle, not the brush!) or cocktail stick and drive your tool through the centre of each ball to make a hole in them. You have now created beads!

These need to dry before putting any essential oil on them, so you can either let them air-dry for 24–48 hours, checking every now and then to see how they are doing, or you can put them into your oven on its lowest setting for 2–3 hours.

Once they are dry, you are ready to thread them onto your fabric. Tie a knot in one end of the fabric. I found the easiest way of threading was to cut the other end of the fabric on an angle to create a fine point, then twist it. You will use this twisted end to poke through the hole.

Once you have threaded on your beads, tie a loop in the top to make it easy to hang.

Now simply drop your essential oil directly onto the beads. They will keep the scent for a little while, and can just top them up when they need it.

Note: If you are pregnant, please only use essential oils if you have checked their suitability.

WHY I LOVE IT

It is not only a treat for yourself, but also a mindful clay-craft. It also makes a lovely gift if paired with some essential oil.

MAKING IT YOUR OWN

If you wanted to turn these into personal scent necklaces, you could choose some lovely string (around 50–60cm in length) and thread your beads onto that before adding the scents.

HOW YOU CAN USE THIS

As well as creating this diffuser for your car or your home, you can also add lavender essential oil and put it in your wardrobes or drawers to deter moths and make your clothes smell good in the process!

(Note: If you are making a diffuser for your car, please make sure you don't use any essential oils that could make you drowsy while driving.)

Botanical Biscuits

· ·

If you're looking to take something to a friend's house for a sweet treat, a gift for a godchild, or to add into a hamper just to make someone smile, then this versatile vegan recipe is a total joy.

I chose to include a baking recipe in this chapter because baking has provided a kind of therapy to many since the beginning of time, and sharing your homemade bakes raises that happiness bar even further! Baking provides us with sensory stimulation, relieves stress and provides a different form of mediation that can slot into a day easily, and benefits not just us, but our loved ones too.

What you will need
Makes 3 large or 6 medium biscuits

Edible flowers, pressed briefly before use (for example violas, calendula, nasturtium, borage, dianthus, marigolds)

50g soft brown sugar

150g plain flour, plus more for dusting your surface

Mixing bowl

100g vegan butter, cubed

Zest of 1 lemon

Vanilla extract

Cookie cutter

Baking tray

Baking parchment

Palette knife

Sprinkle of caster sugar

Optional: A piece of cardboard (cut into a square the same size as your biscuits), butchers' string, Kraft label

Method

Heat the oven to 180°C/160°C Fan/gas mark 4.

Put your edible flowers underneath a chopping board or books, to press slightly, as it will be easier to put them onto the biscuits if they are flatter.

Mix the sugar and flour in a bowl and add the cubed butter. With clean fingers, rub together the mixture until it resembles breadcrumbs. Add the lemon zest and vanilla extract and go through a few more times with your fingertips. Once the mixture starts to come together, you can tip it onto a clean, floured surface, then work the crumb until it is a dough. You want to be able to roll it out without it breaking, but don't overwork it, otherwise the butter will get too sticky (if this happens, add a little more flour).

Break the dough into three balls, then, rather than using a rolling pin, I use the heel of my hand to press it out to around 0.5cm thickness. Get a large cookie cutter to shape the dough and keep any leftovers to the side in case you want to make some extra small biscuits.

Line a baking tray with parchment. Now get your edible flowers from their makeshift press and start to arrange them on top of the biscuits, pressing them in carefully (you may need to press petals in individually). Use a palette knife to carefully lift the biscuits onto a baking tray, leaving about 2cm between each biscuit as they are likely to spread a little once in the oven.

I bake mine for 15 minutes, but I recommend checking them after 10 minutes to make sure they are baking evenly.

Pull them out the oven and sprinkle a little caster sugar over the biscuits and leave to cool on the tray for 30 minutes or longer, before lifting them off. If you lift them off too early, they will break . . . lesson learnt!

If you would like to wrap the biscuits up as a gift, cut out a piece of cardboard the size of your biscuits, then place your biscuits in a tower on top. Now get a large piece of baking parchment and wrap the biscuits neatly, using string to tie it up, then finally add a gift tag.

WHY I LOVE IT

My baking is a bit hit or miss, but this is really successful and simple recipe that will be enjoyed by vegans and non-vegans alike. Relaxation can be found in the kneading of the dough and creative expression can be unleashed on this big, edible canvas!

HOW YOU CAN USE THIS

Obviously these can be consumed immediately with a cup of tea, but I have also made them up to serve as individual desserts with a little scoop of ice cream, or added to the side of a posset. Gifting these might be hard, but your recipient is sure to enjoy them.

MAKING IT YOUR OWN

If you are making this in the autumn or winter months and edible flowers are out of season, then think about ways you can use seasonal flavourings like cinnamon, orange zest, a little added cocoa powder, chocolate drops or ginger. This is a great base recipe and lends itself very well to variations.

Pressed Flower Candles

· ·

Elegant and easy to make, you can apply this method to tapered candles or pillar candles as well as electric candles made from real wax. They add life to a table setting or celebration, and you can simply wrap one up in a little baking parchment to give to a loved one.

What you will need

Makes 1 pillar candle

Lighter/matches

A cream pillar candle (and another candle for heating the knife)

Small hand towel

Selection of pressed flowers (choose the flattest ones for this, see page 166)

Baking parchment

A butter knife

Kraft label

Method

Light a candle and keep it to the side; this will be used to heat your butter knife shortly. Use the hand towel like a pillow to secure your candle so it doesn't roll around and you can have both hands free.

Place your pressed flowers onto the pillar candle decoratively and then put the baking parchment over the top. Carefully hold your knife over the flame of the other candle and leave it for about 30 seconds (be careful of fingers!). Then bring it over to the parchment and touch gently down over the pressed flowers with the hot part of the knife. Try not to go too much beyond the flower onto the candle as all the wax around it will melt too. Using a knife gives you more precision, but the tip of an iron also works (I tried this in the process and was equally pleased with the results). Peel the parchment off, turn the candle and work your way around with your pattern of flowers. The pressed flowers will have been held in place by the melted wax.

Wrap the candle in a little parchment and seal with a Kraft label to gift to friends.

Note: As with all candles, please do not leave unattended once lit.

WHY I LOVE IT

This is a great craft to use up some of the pressed flowers you might find between your books after being inspired in Chapter 2 (see page 72). It makes a pillar candle really stand out and takes no time at all.

HOW YOU CAN USE THIS

This makes a wonderful table decoration; simply add a single candle to a small plate or put three different sizes onto a wooden chopping board for a centrepiece.

MAKING IT YOUR OWN

Use individual petals or leaves to create a mandala pattern on the candle. Keep the candle steady with the hand towel and create the design first, before covering in baking parchment and gently heating with the butter knife as above.

Salt-Dough Tags

· ·

Salt dough is not just for kids and Christmas – it is satisfying to make, it feels nostalgic and is a traditional craft that has been around since Ancient Egyptian times! It is made with just three ingredients: flour, water and salt, which acts as a preservative. Salt dough became a trend in the seventies when people made salt-dough figurines and wreaths that would sometimes be coloured and glazed to hang up in the home or, as was made popular in Germany, created as a celebratory offering and tree ornaments at Christmas.

What you will need
Makes 15 small tags

1 cup plain flour, plus more for dusting your work surface

¼ cup fine salt

Mixing bowl

¼ cup warm water

Knife or shaped cookie cutters

Baking tray

Paper straw

Twine or string

Optional: Watercolour paints, fine-liner pens, craft varnish
(I like Mod-podge)

Method

Heat your oven to its lowest setting (around 140°C/120°C Fan/gas mark 1), then measure out your ingredients. Put the flour and salt into a mixing bowl, slowly pour in the warm water and combine.

Once your doughy ball is forming, take it out and pop it onto a very lightly floured surface and knead like you would if making bread.

Roll out the dough, not too thinly, and using your knife, cut out small rectangle tag shapes, or use the cookie cutter to press out your shapes.

Lay all your shapes out on the baking tray and punch a hole in each one using a straw where you would like to thread it onto twine or string. Be sure not to punch your hole too close the edge, otherwise it might break. Pop the baking tray into the heated oven for around 3 hours. Set an alarm and check them at 45-minute intervals, turning them over so they dry on both sides.

Once they are dry you can thread the string through the holes. You could use watercolour paints or a fine-liner pen to decorate, or you could coat them in a water-based, craft varnish like Mod-podge.

WHY I LOVE IT

I love making dough; kneading and moulding, using my hands in this relaxing and meditative craft to unwind and find a moment of peace in a primal activity. Using our hands in this way is proven to help us relieve stress, anxiety and find flow.[11]

HOW YOU CAN USE THIS

You can use these as gift tags, name places on napkin rings and ornaments to hang on Christmas trees or for Easter celebrations.

MAKING IT YOUR OWN

If you have any block stamps with patterns, images or letters, you can press these into your salt dough before putting them in the oven. This is great for a really personal touch to your name tag or table setting.

A Hand-Painted Plant Pot

· ·

I love gardening. I enjoy flowers, and nature is essential to my well-being, but indoor plants seem to be where I meet my limit, and I have found I am not so green-fingered when it comes to keeping the home alive with greenery, tropicals and succulents. You may wonder why, then, I am encouraging you to make and gift a potted plant for a loved one?

Well, first, not everyone is like me, and I watch in awe as aficionados like Angela Maynard of Botany in East London present a dining table's worth of living, thriving, lush indoor greenery with ease and elegance. Secondly, fusing it with a creative activity such as painting and personalizing the pot gives it that extra level of nurturing and care that one might need to fully invest in the well-being of the plant. You could also choose to pot an outdoor plant, a hardy herb or some spring bulbs – all things I'm much better at!

Write a little note for your gift's recipient on how to look after their new friend and hope that it will encourage more of us to fill our spaces with green, life-giving flora!

What you will need
Makes 1 painted pot

Terracotta pot with saucer (or some pebbles if no saucer)

Acrylic paint (water-resistant if to be used outdoors; you will need white for a base coat)

Paintbrush

A plant

Some potting soil

Optional: Masking or Washi tape, a pencil

Method

First you need to apply a base coat to your chosen pot. Terracotta pots are porous and some paint will soak into them, so adding a base coat of white acrylic paint makes decorating them with patterns, symbols or pictures much smoother, and colours will stand out more too.

Create a whitewash by wetting your paintbrush and dabbing it into the white acrylic paint, then gently cover your entire pot with a thin layer. You can decide whether you want to paint the inside and the base, though it's not essential. If your pot has come with a saucer, then whitewash that too. Leave it to dry for an hour.

Whatever you choose to have as the main colours in the background, you can now paint these on. For multi-layered designs, my recommendation is to go for lighter background colours, so that any foreground images will stand out. Masking tape or Washi tape can be used to create lines and block colours and won't take off the base paint. Leave layers of paint to dry before adding anything on top.

If you want to add designs or pictures to the pot, you can always draw them on first with a pencil and fill them in with the paint. Use layers when adding detail – if I want to draw yellow seeds on a strawberry,

I might do a little dot of white first, then layer a dot of yellow on top, as this gives some depth.

When choosing your designs, think about the occasion, the season you are in or the person you are giving it to, as these will really be the best guides for your project.

Once the paint on your pot has completely dried, it's time to fill it with potting soil, or some earth from your own garden. If you have a saucer then you can put a little base soil straight into the pot. For an outdoors plant if you have a drainage hole but no saucer, then you can put a few pebbles in the bottom of the pot. This will hold the soil but still allow water to drain out when you water your plant.

If you are taking a plant from a container to repot, gently ease it out with all the roots and then give it a little shake over a bowl. Put the plant,

roots and attached soil into your new pot of soil and nestle it in with your fingers. Add soil around it, pat down and repeat until the plant is secure and the roots are bedded in. If you are using bulbs, then follow the packet instructions in in terms of how many you'll need for your pot size.

Give the plant a little water and then add a label to tell the person you will be giving it to how to care for their new plant.

WHY I LOVE IT

A really easy and cheering gift. As much as I love a bunch of flowers, this makes a change and offers a chance for a friend to nurture something and watch it bloom and grow. Of course, the pot is re-usable too, so it can be used for more plant loving or to keep your wooden spoons in by the cooker!

HOW YOU CAN USE THIS

Choose an easy-to-care-for herb plant or flowering plant to put into your pot. Gift it to a neighbour, or create a few with positive messages to put outside your gate, door, or in a local spot for people to take as a gift from a stranger!

MAKING IT YOUR OWN

You could make little plant name markers for your pot. Take a small ball of air-dry clay (I use Das Clay), roll it out, cut it into the shape of a marker and leave it to dry for 24 hours. Coat with a water-resistant seal (I use Mod-Podge varnish), write on it in Sharpie pen then dig it into the front area of the plant so it's visible.

An Invitation . . .
To Gather

I left the activities in this last chapter purposefully open-ended and less directive than the other prompts in the book. That is because the action of gathering – the process, the planning, leaving your comfort zone and being in a creative space – is more of a prescription for your well-being than anything else. We come together to be within a community, to feel the radiating effect of positivity found by sharing our feelings, stories and thoughts with one another. Not only does connection make us feel rejuvenated mentally and physically, it can also provide us with opportunities to commune with like-minded people. It won't always feel easy. In fact, it is often very hard to go out, to log in or to be around others. Sometimes it feels like the last thing you want . . . but that's actually when you need it the most.

My intention in this chapter is to offer you the guidance needed to co-ordinate a gathering with a difference, with helpful hints and things I have learned from working with groups myself and navigating being a beginner among others. The activities can be used as the central focus of a social event, or as an ice-breaker when meeting new friends, as well as to make connections around the world with clubs and events online when you can't meet in real life.

What I really love about crafting in a group is the strong sense that I am participating in an ancient tradition. To not only be together, but be doing and making with each other, feels nurturing and comforting in a way that can only come from a much deeper inner knowledge of its power. Our creativity has the potential to flow with more ease in a forum, as does our sense of purpose, and I hope you will come to discover that there are many different and unusual ways to hang out, even for those quieter friends among us.

Quick Inspiration

. . . .

STARTING A CRAFT CLUB

All it takes to start a club is one person, one idea and one invite. In early 2021, missing my social life and feeling full of inspiration, I sent out such an invite to see if anyone wanted to join me online to get crafty and try some making activities with me. I wrote down a plan to cover five weeks, sent out a materials list and a Zoom link, then, come Saturday evenings at 8pm, we would meet, drink of choice in hand, and I'd lead a workshop in candles or DIY beauty products, and more. I chose crafts that I wanted to try out personally and worked out which experiences might be best for a group setting, albeit online. A craft club, different to a typical book-club format, is a space where you can be together to do something practical – discussing it, asking questions, sharing in your own achievements and honouring the things that didn't work out as planned . . . embracing all of that with fun, joy and laughter!

With all the same excitable nerves of hosting a dinner party (but with much less mess), I can confirm that these evenings succeeded in bringing together a group of like-minded people from a variety of locations far and wide. Everyone embraced being creative, being a beginner, and was totally accepting of whatever the outcome, with all the mistakes that might come along the way.

You might live somewhere far from your friends and need a reason to connect regularly, or you might have moved somewhere new, looking for a way to meet people. If so, this is a great place to start!

Here are a few tips on how to begin your own creative club . . .

Invite your closest friends and encourage them to pass it on
This will be the way to start your creative community. 'Bring a friend' also works as an idea, and if you are hosting online, you will need to give your online room link to be shared.

Keep it to 2 hours maximum
Think about your time frame when you are choosing your activity, too. For example, consider if it requires any cooking, freezing or drying time.

Prepare the crafts or activities around the season
Thinking about the time of year will bring a harmony to the crafts, including the ease of sourcing materials and ways you can use your crafts afterwards. You can also factor in special festivals or celebrations to inspire and guide you.

Be sustainable where possible
This means using what you have, looking in nature for materials, using recyclables or even repurposing old things. Keep ingredients and materials lists to a minimum.

Welcome everyone
If you are the host, even if it feels a little out of your comfort zone, introduce yourself and say why you want to do this. Ask everyone to say who they are, too, as some people might not know each other.

Learn from each other

In the group dynamic you may find some will know more than others. Offer to help each other, answer questions and research when something isn't known. Learning together will foster safety and enthusiasm.

How to progress the club

If you want to grow your club, then start a page on Instagram or Facebook and put up the dates, venue, craft and materials list and open it up to a wider audience, perhaps a group local to where you live.

A note on costs

When I hosted my club, it was online. I asked everyone to source their own materials and I provided a very detailed list, including what I would be using, or where to buy everything. These were the only costs involved. If you are using a venue that charges, then you might like to ask everyone to contribute to that hire within a ticket price.

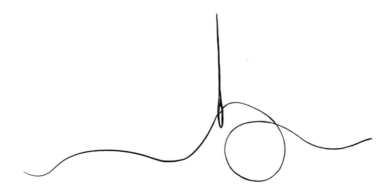

Clay Date Night

. . . .

Two years ago, I booked an evening ceramics workshop for myself and my husband as an alternative date night. After we made miniature cups and saucers for our daughters, we moved on to a grown-up mug and bowl, and even more than that, we both found our love of clay and hanging out in an art room with lovely people and herbal tea!

Working with clay offers an opportunity to find our flow, relax and reflect, as well as having the positive effects of reducing our anxiety and stress levels. It is said that one way of bringing yourself into the present moment, which is the main intention of mindfulness practice, is to focus on our breathing. You can use your time working with clay to help with the rhythm of your breathing . . . which is a great tip to help ease even the most reluctant of clay date-nighters!

What you will need (per person)

1kg pack of air-dry clay in white or terracotta (I use Das Clay)

Damp cloth to wipe hands

Chopping board

Small bowl of water

Mood lighting

Good playlist

Drink of choice

For making a candlestick holder
Candle

For making an ornament
Rolling pin

Butter knife/cookie cutters

Paper straw

Method
Making a pinch pot
Break off a bit of clay (about the size of a ping pong ball) and roll it in the palm of your hand, then press your thumb into the centre of the ball. Using your thumb and index finger, work the edges outwards, turning the clay slowly with your other hand. The ball will start to resemble a small pot, and you can work on this until you are happy with how it looks – just don't over-work it, otherwise it will get too thin and break.

You can leave it the way it is, or you can use your butter knife to gently score in patterns.

Making a candlestick holder
The easiest way of making a candlestick holder is to use a candle to help shape the clay.

Break off some small bits of clay and then roll them into snakes. Wrap them like rings around the candle, one after another, rubbing a drop of water over the clay to help them stick. Go a short way up your candle (about 10cm), then ease your candle out from the centre and let your holder dry out.

Making an ornament

Break off some of your clay and, using your rolling pin, roll it out until it's about 2mm in thickness – any thinner and it will break when it's dried. Now use your butter knife or cookie cutters to cut out shapes. You will need to press a hole into the clay to hang string or ribbon from, and I find a straw good for this.

Pot luck . . .

Get your partner to choose a model-object for you to make . . . it could be one of your pets, a favourite food item, a floral tea light holder or a character!

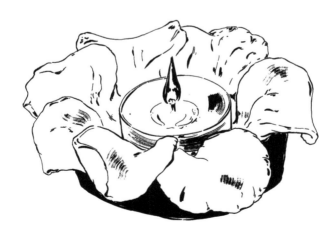

WHY I LOVE IT

I love this activity because there is joy in turning off the TV and hanging out with your loved one, crafting and having a laugh – either because you are enjoying yourselves so much, or because you can't help giggling about your pot-luck figurines! Either way, it's refreshing to change up the way you spend time with one another.

HOW YOU CAN USE THIS

Not only is clay-crafting a very calming activity for yourself, it is a great activity to do while hanging out with a friend, chatting, drinking tea and working with your hands. It brings a focus to a catch-up and really adds joy to a date night, encouraging self-confidence and stimulating our imaginations, making this a brilliant craft to share with someone special.

MAKING IT YOUR OWN

Taking this to the next level would be organizing date night number two as a painting session for your wonderful clay items! You can use acrylic paints with a matte or gloss varnish to give it an expert finish. Remember: you will only be able to put liquid into the pots/vases/cups if you do a full waterproof varnish – inside and outside.

Natural Dyed Socks

· ·

Natural and botanical dyes are surprising, satisfying and have a long history – the use of natural dyes was first recorded as far back as 2600 BCE.[12] I enjoy fabric dying and have often used powder dyes as a way of covering food or drink stains and to simply to give clothes a new lease of life (see ice-dye T-shirts on page 197). I am interested in the mindful and slow-paced process of using natural pigments to create organic, earthy tones. I have played around with colours from a variety of fruits, spices, plants and vegetables and am always fascinated by the sometimes unlikely results: red cabbage staining blue, avocado skins bringing an apricot shade and rich green leaves producing no colour at all.

Natural dying has a place as a communal activity (a nod to traditional crafty gatherings) that can be shared alongside friends. As an entry-level activity, cotton socks are easy to acquire (and the perfect fabric to learn with) and you only need a small number of ingredients. An outfit is always improved by a splash of colour about your ankles!

A note on some natural dyes

Blackberries, beetroot and red cabbage give a very impressive first results – but as they are considered 'stains' they will fade to light grey after a couple of washes.

Won't the colour wash out?

Before proceeding with any dying, we need to 'fix' the fabric so that our colour will hold. In all honesty, this is always the bit I am concerned about and I have failed at previously due to rushing, forgetting and probably secretly believing I didn't need to fix them at all. I now know this is not true and strongly encourage you to pre-treat your fabrics with one of the following methods to give your colours the best chance of fixing to the fabric. A lot of advanced dyers will use a chemical mordant or fixative such as alum or copper which require safety measures and precision but as I am keeping things homespun, we are going to be using things from the kitchen cupboard: vinegar and salt. Materials will all take colours slightly differently, so with this being a natural method do expect variation and some inconsistency.

The first time I did this myself, I had just finished experimenting, labelling and hanging my results up to dry, ready to happily note my findings, when my gang of kittens pulled the drying rack down, mischievously tossing the socks around, leaving them muddled with no telling which was which. The good news is, they were hard to tell apart because they were all successful but for peace of mind I did it all over again and learned a few more tips for you along the way.

How to fix with vinegar for vegetable dyes

Distilled white vinegar will open the fibres of your fabric helping the dye to stick. Use this vinegar solution for all vegetable dyes. Put your pair of socks into a small saucepan, cover with water (around 500ml for 1 pair of sock), then add 1 cup of distilled white vinegar. Bring to the boil, then simmer for 1 hour with a lid on. Drain the vinegar water and, using your tongs (the socks will be hot!), run them under cold water, wring out and put aside ready for the dye. *If you have done this in advance you may need to wet then again with room-temperature water before putting them into your dye solution.*

How to fix with salt

Salt should be used to help your fruit and plant dyes to stick. Put your pair of socks into a small saucepan, cover in water (around 2 cups), then add ½ cup of fine salt. Simmer for 1 hour, then take them out with tongs, run under cold water, wring them out and they are ready to be tied up for dying. *If you have done this in advance you may need to wet then again with room-temperature water before putting them into your dye solution.*

What you will need

For 1 pair of socks

A pair of white cotton socks

Small saucepan

Mixing bowl

Metal or plastic spoon

Tongs

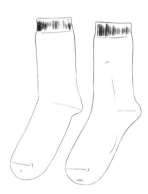

Your natural dye of choice (see pages 190–191)

Optional: Rubber gloves, washing line and pegs or drying rack

Method

I recommend using food-safe items to start with. If you are using plants and botanicals please do make sure you do thorough research to ensure you are not using anything toxic or poisonous. Use a metal or plastic spoon, as wooden spoons will stain.

For deep yellow: 1 tbsp ground turmeric

Put 2 cups of water in a pan and add 1 tbsp of ground turmeric. Stir the until the turmeric is dispersed through the water. Take your pre-fixed socks and make sure they are wet. Fully submerge the socks into the turmeric water, using tongs. Simmer with a lid on for 1 hour, then turn the heat off and leave to soak overnight. The next day, strain your socks into the bowl and immerse them in cool water to wash them, wringing them out until the water runs clear. Finally, hang to dry.

For pastel green: 2 cups of spinach leaves

Put your pre-fixed socks into your pan and cover with 2 cups of water, ensuring they are full submerged. Add the 2 cups of spinach and stir so everything is under the water. Put the lid on a simmer for 1 hour, turning your socks with tongs a few times during this time but remembering to put the lid back on so the water doesn't evaporate. After an hour, turn the heat off and leave overnight. *Follow the same final steps for draining, rinsing and drying as above.*

For rusty orange: 1 cup of yellow onion skins

Put your pre-fixed socks into your pan and cover with 2 cups of water, ensuring they are full submerged. Add in the onion skins and stir so everything is under the water. Put the lid on a simmer for 1 hour, turning your socks with tongs a few times during this time but remembering to put the lid back on so the water doesn't evaporate. After an hour, turn the heat off and leave overnight. *Follow the same final steps for draining, rinsing, and drying as above.*

For light yellow: peel only from 2 oranges

Put your pre-fixed socks into your pan and cover with 2 cups of water, ensuring they are full submerged. Add in the orange peel and stir so everything is under the water. Put the lid on and simmer for 1 hour, turning your socks with tongs a few times during this time but remembering to put the lid back on so the water doesn't evaporate. After an hour, turn the heat off and leave overnight. *Follow the same final steps for draining, rinsing and drying as with the deep yellow method.*

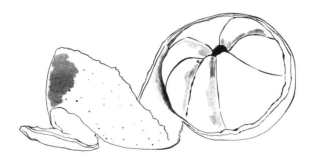

For light grey; 1 cup of blackberries

Put your pre-fixed socks into your pan and cover with 2 cups of water, ensuring they are full submerged. Add in your blackberries and stir so everything is under the water. Put the lid on and simmer for 1 hour, turning your socks with tongs a few times during this time but remembering to put the lid back on so the water doesn't evaporate. After an hour, turn the heat off and leave overnight. *Follow the same final steps for draining, rinsing and drying as with the deep yellow method.*

WHY I LOVE IT

I feel delight at the organic colours that come with this natural method of dying, there is a fulfilment in producing things of beauty from the natural world around us. Also, the aromas are amazing when you are creating the citrus and berry dyes, filling the kitchen with an instant homey atmosphere.

HOW YOU CAN USE THIS

Buy a pack of white cotton socks for a friend as a gift, dye them in fun, experimental colours, roll them up and present them in a box. You can repurpose a shoe box with a little tissue paper and a gift tag.

MAKING IT YOUR OWN

Use these natural colours for tie-dye on your socks. Lie one sock flat, then, starting at the toe end, pinch it together and start to roll the sock inwards like a snail shell, pinching and rotating until it's scrunched and coiled. Place an elastic band around it tightly to hold it all together, then another one the other way so it's like a cross. Do this for both socks. Then follow the colouring method as on pages 190–191.

Sociable Still Life

The last time I was with a group of girlfriends (before the world went into the pandemic) was a gathering I had organized at my home with ten friends, most of whom didn't know each other well or at all. The theme was a 'sociable still life'. I didn't know how it would work out as it was quite spontaneous, but I knew I wanted to provide an environment that was about gathering and doing something different away from busy jobs and parenthood. I set up a few different spaces with one canvas per friend and then created a floral still life using props. There were cheeseboards, drinks and a variety of mediums, from paint to magazine cut-outs for collage so everyone could choose at their leisure. It was a beautiful evening and took the edge off the usual need for ice-breakers!

I'd suggest this to anyone who wants to have a go at creating a get-together that feels good for the soul and for creative flow.

What you will need (per person)

A canvas

A paintbrush

A small pot of water

A piece of kitchen roll

And for the table . . .

A roll of brown paper

Flowers to arrange

Quirky props; things you can find in nature or around the house

Snacks like a cheeseboard, fruit, vegetables, crisps and dips

Scissors to share

Acrylic or watercolour paint selection

Magazines for collage

Glue sticks to share

Method

This is a very free-style activity. I will advise you on how I built my still life, but you can put your own vision into practice.

First, choose your space – perhaps your dining table – then start to build your still life 'focal point' down the centre. Make sure everyone has a comfy seat. If it is too squashed, think about using another space in addition.

Put down brown paper across the table. This will help with spillages and doodles, and makes everything easier to clean up at the end. You and your guests can also use the paper as your palette too.

You need to have something interesting or colourful for each person to see. Put tall vases of flowers down the centre of the table, and fill these with tall stems and willowy greenery. If you are using candles (electric or real), place these between the vases, staggering the heights (I use cream pillar candles then tealight candles around the edges) and, if using real ones, make sure they are not touching the flowers or greenery for safety.

Now, in the gaps, place props – these can be anything that you think makes it quirky or catches the eye and will add something special to everyone's still life. From interesting glassware to jars or tins of feathers, kids' toys, kitchen utensils, teapots and baskets, choose items with interesting textures, different heights and shapes.

You can now place your drinks (bottles of juice or wine, jugs with waters), a glass per person and a chopping board of snacks (I went with cheese, grapes, fruit and biscuits) on the table. Provide some small plates and cutlery if needed.

Finally, add in the creative materials – sharing jars of scissors, paints and old magazines for cuttings. In front of each guest's place setting, put a canvas, a small pot of water and a paintbrush along with a piece of kitchen roll for cleaning the brush.

Invite your guests to settle into their space and capture whatever it is they can see in front of them. Ask them to accept that elements of the view will change if people are eating and drinking and to incorporate the movement and change into their artwork if necessary. They can get close up, or capture the perspective from afar – the most important thing is to have fun with it. There are no mistakes, so if they do something they want to change, perhaps instead encourage them to work with it and make it a feature of their artwork.

Collage is a lovely introduction for those who are worried about putting brush to canvas, so I recommend having some options for this nearby, from magazines to newspapers. Because the theme is 'what is in front of them', guests won't need to feel worried about plucking a theme from thin air. Encourage guests to seek contrast and go with their initial impulse and not to overthink it. Remind them to notice texture, colour and shape and that they are free to add words too.

Before the evening is out, when everyone is feeling comfortable, happy, socialized and creative, have the group present their paintings for all to see and offer the chance for guests to talk about their piece if they'd like.

WHY I LOVE IT

I find that having a focus in a social environment eases my anxiety, increases my flow and provides the sort of busyness that my hands need to fully relax into a situation.

HOW YOU CAN USE THIS

A birthday, a Sunday lunch, an afternoon tea – this can also be a great way to meet new friends or for a different type of family reunion. There are no limits on when to use this.

MAKING IT YOUR OWN

You could offer everyone the chance to do an artwork swap at the end of the evening. This will bring about a sense of skill-sharing, community and confidence building.

Ice Dye T-Shirts

If it is a joyful item of clothing you are looking for, then a brightly coloured, ice dye T-shirt is the way to go! I wore mine in the last weeks of summer and it gave me all the vibrancy and sunshine that was needed in those days by the seaside. I find this method easier than tie-dye and the effects made by the melting ice are so beautiful. It is a brilliant spring or summer activity to do by yourself or in a group, and you can use natural plant and vegetable dyes or natural powdered colours instead of shop-bought dye. If you are doing this in the colder months, then you can use snow instead of ice . . . a great family activity for the winter!

What you will need
Makes 1 T-shirt

A plain white, cotton T-shirt

Wire rack

Baking tray

A big bowl of ice cubes

Powdered fabric dyes

Rubber gloves

Optional: Elastic bands

Method

I fixed my T-shirt first, so that the dye would hold well. I used a cold-water soak, where you submerge your item in cold water and leave for 20 minutes to fix it. You can read about other fixing methods on page 188.

You can use a tie-dye method of bunching, rolling and tying your T-shirt with elastic bands (see page 192), but it is not essential and, having tried both methods, I was just as happy scrunching up my T-shirt.

Place a wire rack (I use a cake cooling rack) on top of a baking tray – this is so the dye can drip off and it won't soak your garment.

Now place your scrunched-up T-shirt onto the wire rack and cover completely in ice cubes.

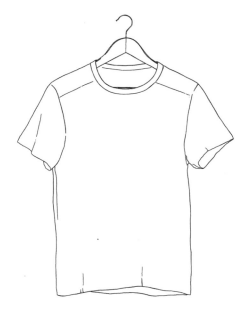

Sprinkle roughly a tablespoon of each colour of dye powder you want to use over the ice, and leave the whole thing until the ice has completely melted. It might take 30 minutes to 1 hour, depending on how warm it is where you are. Leave the T-shirt for another hour with the dye on before rinsing it. The longer you leave it, the deeper the colours will be.

Once you are ready, put the gloves on and pour away the dye water, then rinse your coloured T-shirt under the cold tap until the water runs clear, wringing it out along the way. After I had rinsed it out, I popped it onto a 20-minute cold wash (on its own) and then hung it up to dry in the sunshine!

WHY I LOVE IT

This really is a perfect introduction to dying fabrics and jazzing up your own clothes. The method is incredibly simple, with no complicated instructions so it's great for all ages and skill levels.

HOW YOU CAN USE THIS

Other than using this method on cotton T-shirts, you can also dye your own silk scarves or blankets, canvas shopping bags, cushion covers or baby muslins.

MAKING IT YOUR OWN

Why not add a little embroidered initial, symbol or word to your T-shirt afterwards in complementary straight stitch?

A Terrarium Party

. . . .

A terrarium is an indoor plant container which is either closed or sheltered in some way to create the environment of a miniature green house with the addition of sunlight and water.

The main inspiration for this came when I set up a mini terrarium (or 'little world') workshop for my daughter's second birthday. The kids loved it and I watched on thinking, I want to have another go at this! For the mini versions, I used Mason jars and added in some dinosaurs and farm animals, but I will keep it a little more grown-up here, so it's completely up to you to decide what you include!

I love anything that can be enjoyed in a group and is really easily prepped beforehand, as well as there being beautiful items to take home at the end of it. I read that displaying your own crafts around your home or workshop can actually inspire productivity and boost confidence, as well as generating satisfaction.[13]

What you will need (per person)
Makes 1 terrarium

A wide glass vase (rounded at top) or glass container with lid

Spoon

Fine gravel

Potting soil

Succulent plants, such as jade, hens and chicks, stonecrop, plush plant, Dudleya

Medium-sized pebbles

Sheet moss or tropical moss (optional; see Tip on page 124)

Water spray

Optional: 1 tray per person, roll of brown paper for the table, props of your choice

Method

Set out your materials per guest at a table before they arrive. If you are worried about mess, then place all the items on one tray per person or put brown paper down as a tablecloth. You can put the plants in the middle of the table and have friends choose the own, or you can do this for them.

To make your terrarium, start by spooning the gravel and soil into your chosen glass container – you can do this artistically and create multiple layers which you will see through the glass, or you can simply do one then the other. You will want to plant into the soil, however, so just make sure that this forms the topmost layer.

If the plants are in bigger pots or multipacks, then gently tease the plants out of the soil, shake off the excess, trim any very long roots and separate them if they are joined on to others.

Nestle the plants into the soil layer in your glass, then decoratively arrange the fine gravel or medium pebbles around it. You can also place moss over the soil areas, which will also help to hold in moisture. In terms of filling your container, you want to be working up to the halfway point, so that there is still plenty of space above.

Finally, add your props if using them and add a little spritz of water. Keep a water spray to hand, as this will be the best way to keep your terrarium alive and well, without overwatering your plants.

> **Tip:** The putting-together can be as intricate as you like, and for more precise planting and decorating, you can use tweezers.

WHY I LOVE IT

I am a self-confessed beginner at indoor plants, but this is easy to care for and also makes a great gift for someone who might also like some low-maintenance greenery for their home.

HOW YOU CAN USE THIS

Your terrarium can be displayed in your home, on a windowsill or on your desk at work to bring some life to your surroundings. It can also be set up as a really enjoyable group activity around the kitchen table.

MAKING IT YOUR OWN

Add some little props or foraged items into your terrarium, such as special crystals, painted pebbles or hand-written positive messages.

Marbling Mailouts

. . . .

I tried this out with my best friends for one of their birthdays online, and it was certainly a learning curve! One of my friends was so worried about the mess she covered herself in bin liners, another was secretly googling easier ways of marbling (trying not to offend me), while yet another was disappointed hers weren't working out. Meanwhile, all of us were exclaiming, 'Was marbling always this hard?' as we drank in celebration and communal creativity! It was funny and challenging,

but the main thing was that it got us all together, focusing on a task, even though we were miles apart.

We went into this with minimal to no experience yet I was still surprised at how shy people are to own their beautiful work and share their creativity with confidence; that some of us feel we have failed when something doesn't turn out how we expect right away. The biggest lesson for me as the host of this 'online craft party' was the need to try to encourage a different mindset – one of accomplishment, even with the difficulties.

In sharing this activity with you, I have tweaked a couple of aspects, but I absolutely stand by the fact that receiving a craft pack and having a date in the diary to do this with others brings absolute joy, and I can't wait for you to try it.

What you will need

A set of marbling paints (see Note below)

Selection of paper, notecards and envelopes

Baking parchment

Toothpick

Padded envelope (for the mailout)

Rubber gloves

Baking tray or deep dish

Kitchen roll or a tea towel

Optional: roll of brown paper for the table, aprons

Which marbling paints should I use?

Before we start, please note that this is an introduction to marbling, intended for groups at any skill level. As a beginner myself in many things, I've found the best way to entice me to go further or commit to the activity is to set the level at achievable . . . so that is why I recommend looking for kids' marbling paints. These will still achieve an amazing effect without overly complicated instructions. If you have much more experience, then please do use more advanced marbling inks and tools.

Method

For a mailout to friends

Pop 2 or 3 marbling inks along with your paper selection, a piece of baking parchment and a toothpick into a padded envelope, and send this out to each friend. Create a link to join a private online room by email with the instructions that they should prepare themselves with a drink, a pair of rubber gloves and a deep dish filled with room temperature water. They should have their envelope of treats to hand!

For an in-person session

Prepare the space for your friends at a well-protected table (you could use brown paper to cover the surface). Each participant should have all the tools above and they may like to wear an apron and gloves. Put the inks in the middle for everyone to share and similarly spread the papers out for them to choose from.

Now for the messy bit . . .

Get your tray of water and sporadically drop a little marbling ink into it. You can use one colour or a few. It will naturally spread around and make shapes, but you can also use the toothpick to drag through the paints and create a feathered effect.

Now place your paper carefully on top of the water, being careful not to let the paper be submerged. After you have placed the entire sheet down on the surface of the water, you can immediately start to peel it off again very carefully and place it onto your baking parchment to dry. Your kitchen roll or tea towel will be handy for any spills but you can also use the kitchen roll to clean your water surface and start again.

WHY I LOVE IT

Marbling is nostalgic. It takes some practise, but even the results of trial and error look exquisite. Sending a little pack out to friends is such a lovely way of communing from afar.

HOW YOU CAN USE THIS

As well as sending out to friends, this can easily be set up for an in-person group too. A perfect get-together, with results that dry in minimal time. The marbling effect makes a magical invite, set of notecards or name-place cards as well as gift tags for presents and wrapping paper.

MAKING IT YOUR OWN

Zeena Shah (@heartzeena), the master of art direction and marbling, recommends trying this method out on glass. Simply roll a glass bottle, vase or jar around the marbling ink and let it dry to create a very different and very professional-looking decorative vase or candle holder.

Jam-Jar Ice Creams

. . . .

This is not strictly a craft, but if we want to find joy in making (and eating!), gathering and discovering new ways to create brilliant, easy, communal things, then this is as good an activity as any! My friend mentioned 'jam-jar ice creams' and I had honestly never heard of them before, but then I went on such a journey with the many incredible blogs and recipe pages that do all sorts of variations on these. My husband is vegan and my kids mostly eat vegan too, so I decided to try this with a non-dairy product.

What you will need
Makes 1 x 250ml jam-jar ice cream (or 2 x 125ml jars)

A clean and dry Mason jar (freezer-proof)

125ml non-dairy whipping cream

1½ tsp vanilla extract

1½ tsp caster sugar

A sticker and a pen or a coloured ribbon

Optional extras: sprinkles, fresh crushed raspberries, fresh chopped-up strawberries, jam, peanut butter, crushed-up chocolate bars

Method

This is a great activity to do at a party with a group of friends, but, as it will need to freeze for 3 hours, I'd suggest making this the first thing you do (the 'ice-breaker'). In the meantime, there will be plenty of time to chat, eat and dance before dessert!

Set out a Mason jar per person, with the ingredients measured out, then put sharing bowls of extra bits in the middle of the table so people add a little of what they fancy. Next, put on a great playlist: you will be shaking this jar for a solid 2 minutes, so you want to be doing it to a good song! Everyone can label their own jar, or you can use ribbon to tell them apart, tied around the neck of the jar.

Put all of your ingredients, including any extras you might like to add into your ice-cream mix, fix the lid on the jar securely, set a timer for

2 minutes and shake vigorously non-stop. At some point you will hear the cream change from a liquid to a heavier sound in the jar, and it will feel different too, which is great as that means it is thickening up.

With your newly pumped muscles, place all the jars in the freezer and allow the magic to happen!

When you return to your jars you will be surprised and thrilled to find a soft, cloudy, creamy iced dessert . . . no doubt leaving friends feeling inspired to try this again at home!

WHY I LOVE IT

Other than the fact that this is the only arm workout I'm getting, I feel it really helps ease people into a social situation. Having a focus that seems a bit like a wacky experiment is the sort of playful prompt that not many of us find in our daily life. Also, it tastes delicious.

HOW YOU CAN USE THIS

Ideal for a summer get-together, movie night or birthday weekend with a bunch of friends, this is also a great activity to try with your family – the kids will love it!

MAKING IT YOUR OWN

You can use dairy whipping or heavy cream for this if you prefer. There are so many flavour varieties to try, but my absolutely favourite is this one:

Open up the jar, straight from the freezer and add some optional toppings like chopped walnuts and chopped banana, pour over some warm chocolate sauce – and you have a banana split in a jar either for sharing or just for you!

An Embroidery Circle

· ·

There is something about being in a group of people in a circle – be that to talk, to craft, to play or to share – that feels sacred. There is a sense of safety from outside threats and distractions, with space inside to be. A circle also helps to create a central focus. While researching group circles, I read that circles 'can be widened to accommodate more and narrowed when people leave',[14] which I thought was a beautiful way of conveying the group's ability to welcome and accept as well as be flexible.

Crafting together, especially for the first time, can be daunting, but embroidery has been proven time and time again to have therapeutic qualities, bringing us into the present. Needlework is used often in the treatment of those suffering with mental health issues and to help people overcome trauma, and was even used after the First World War to help soldiers suffering with shellshock.[15] No matter what your mental health status, however, I really encourage you to try sitting in one of these welcoming embroidery circles, if only for the opportunity to switch off from the fast-moving, high-tech world around you.

What you will need

Embroidery thread

Scissors

Needles

Embroidery rings (any size)

Fabric square (cut bigger than the ring you are using)

Pencils

Optional: Books/images for reference and inspiration

Method

Please use this method as a guide for how to organize and get started with this group. You can show an example of the 4 types of stitch on page 214 but you should theme these groups however you like. The idea with this activity is to get a group together and benefit from the process of needlework – anything that comes as a result of the group is a side note to the sense of togetherness and self-care born from the doing.

When choosing a theme (e.g. 'Botanical'), bring books or images for reference. This will help people plan their designs, symbols or patterns.

Make sure there is good lighting; seats should be comfortable and upright. Try to do a little Q&A so that when you start to stitch, you can really relax into it. A little break in the middle of the session is also advisable. If you are doing this in the summer months, then I recommend doing this outside on blankets, sitting in a circle together.

Put all the thread is some baskets and add to the table with a jar of scissors, some needles and an embroidery ring for each person. They can bring their own fabric or you can provide them with a piece to start off.

Show the group how to get started by cutting a piece of embroidery thread around 30cm (if its too long it will tangle!) then tie a double knot in the end of it. They will then want to find their starting position of choice on the fabric and pull their needle and thread up through the fabric from the back of the ring until you reach the knot, which ensures your thread is secure to continue stitching. At the end of using that specific colour, they need to push the thread through to the back of the fabric and tie a double knot in the back, close to the fabric as possible. Remove the needle, put it somewhere safe, then cut any trailing thread to finish.

Before the session ends, go around the circle and ask everyone how they feel and offer everyone the opportunity to show their efforts to the group.

WHY I LOVE IT

Embroidery busies hands, providing a creative outlet as well as helping to encourage connection.

HOW YOU CAN USE THIS

Use embroidery as part of your own creative 'soul care' or start a group locally. If this is a one-off for a bridal party, birthday or Christmas craft-a-long, then keep it simple to appeal to all skill levels and set the theme!

MAKING IT YOUR OWN

If you want to bring the group together even more and work on a collective project, then you could all meet over several weeks, each working on squares to put together as a special quilt. You can incorporate buttons, beads and different fabric patches too, for those who want to go beyond the beginner's stitch techniques.

Basic embroidery stitch ideas

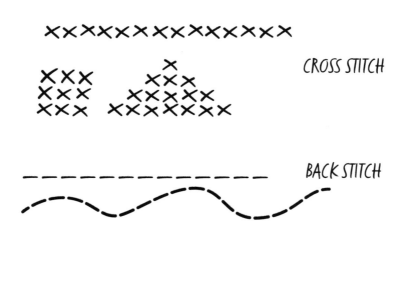

CROSS STITCH

BACK STITCH

RUNNING STITCH

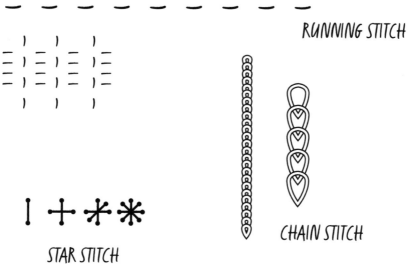

CHAIN STITCH

STAR STITCH

Decoupage . . . Anything!

Decoupage is the cutting, layering and varnishing of paper cut-outs onto items and, for me, it will always feel nostalgic. It reminds me of my sister, as I watched in awe of her artistic creations through the nineties and of her Victorian decoupage book, brimming with delicate roses and porcelain hands. I was more into cut-outs of Take That members from *Top of the Pops* magazine – hardly elegant decoupage but similarly enticing – stuck onto anything from wastepaper baskets to plates and trinket boxes.

This is a wonderful group activity, to be incorporated into crafts for celebrations, upcycling or just for some 'you' time. Paper-cutting is also a great form of mindfulness, as you focus completely on the task at hand.

What you will need

Paper-cutting scissors

Old magazines, decoupage book, old wrapping paper or paper napkins

An object to cover

PVA or spray glue

Sponge brush/paintbrush

A clean, dry sponge

Craft varnish (I like Mod-podge)

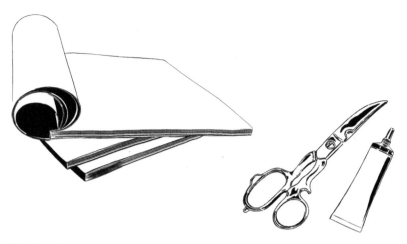

Method

Whatever materials you are using, the method will be the same, though if you are using paper napkins, which work really well, they may take handling with a little more delicacy. I will guide you here with some tips to make the experience of decoupage as open-ended and effortless as possible. If you are doing this as a group, please ensure everyone has their own scissors and a comfortable chair to sit on at a table.

Work in a clear workspace and whatever your chosen object, make sure that you will be sticking onto a clean and flat surface area.

With any cutting, I usually cut around the picture quickly first before going into it in much more detail – it is much easier this way as you won't have to hold a heavy magazine or large piece of paper at an awkward angle.

If you have a design in mind, this is the time to plan that out. You may like to cut out all your pieces first if this is the case.

Apply glue to your cut-out with a sponge brush or a paintbrush then place the cut-out onto the object you are covering. Once on, use your dry sponge to smooth out any creases and get rid of air bubbles. Repeat this process with the rest of your sticking.

Once everything is set in place, let it dry completely, then cover your object in craft glue or varnish. You'll want to do a few layers, letting each one dry before adding another. Everything should be sealed and feel smooth and as one, like the pictures are embedded into the object.

WHY I LOVE IT

The cutting and sticking is a form of meditation. It brings you into a slower pace, concentrating only on what's in front of you.

HOW YOU CAN USE THIS

Elaborating on a few ideas from this book, decoupage will work really well on your DIY Party Crackers (page 139), Punched-Hole Lanterns (page 132) or your Hand Painted Plant Pot (page 174).

MAKING IT YOUR OWN

This is already a unique craft, as each thing you create has the potential to be wildly different. To think about how you can use this method elsewhere. Perhaps try to think outside the box: can you do the inside of a drawer to add a quirk to a piece of furniture? Or maybe the inside of a gift box if giving to a friend? Print your own pictures onto suitable paper and try that out – decoupage glue and varnish won't smudge the photo ink. You can also use craft varnish to decoupage fabric!

References

1   positivepsychology.com/flow-activities/

2   researchgate.net/publication/235955024_Crafts_as_a_way_to_
    functional_mental_health

3   bbc.co.uk/news/entertainment-arts-48188508

4   doseofnature.org.uk

5   theconversation.com/the-surprising-science-of-fidgeting-77525

6   positivepsychology.com/benefits-of-journaling/

7   nationalpeaceacademy.us/images/files/children/YOUTH-3-v1.pdf

8   indiaflint.com/ecoprint

9   verywellmind.com/stress-helping-others-can-increase-
    happiness-3144890

10 gov-online.go.jp/eng/publicity/book/hlj/html/202009/202009_07_
    en.html

11 insidehighered.com/blogs/gradhacker/make-things-your-hands

12 researchgate.net/publication/321157082_Natural_Dye_-_Ancient_and_
    Contemporary_Context

13 bebrainfit.com/benefits-art/

14 groupworksdeck.org/patterns/Circle

15 crewelwork.com/blogs/news/world-mental-health-day-embroidery-as-
    therapy

Acknowledgements

To my husband Russell and daughters, Mabel and Peggy. You give me so much inspiration and joy everyday. I love you so much.

Alice and my Found family, thank you for all the dedicated attention, for listening to my lengthy voice notes and giving me the space to be totally myself while guiding me gently through this project and more.

Francesca, for everything over the years and for introducing me to Found. It will always be more than fine!

Carole as always for believing in me. It means so much to me and gives me a confidence that I didn't know I had!

Martha for your hard work on this book and for coming into it with such enthusiasm and a keen eye.

To all at Bluebird; Jess, Mel and Jodie for bringing fun, spirit and creativity to all that you do.

To Mereki. For our walks, when I've needed to get out and clear my head or when I just wanted to pick up the phone, you have been there and present and it's much appreciated.

India for always thinking of me when you see creative projects, keep sending me prompts and inspiration! I trust you totally.

To my mum, dad, Jamie, Kirsty and Erika, Oscar and Jude for all the family joy, since forever.

Rosie! Your positivity and words or wisdom carry me when I need them. Also for your mutual love of marathon-voice notes.

Lara, Sophie, Charlotte, Emily and Molly as always. For support, love, laughter.

To Alicia and the team, you are all crucial to the smooth sailing of a home and work balance. Thank you.

To Jerome! For fixing my back! So I was able to continue writing this book and living a pain-free life!

Manya for years of support and being there for me, without fail!

Lisa M, you are helping me to really get to know myself. You are a huge inspiration to me as I know you are to many other women and mothers.

Fearne you work harder than any other I know as a creative person, artist, mother, wife and great human. Thank you for supporting this book as you did my first.

Melissa, you bring joy to our kitchen daily and I am truly grateful and honoured that you would be a part of this book. Thank you.

Resources

BOOKS

Decorative Dough Craft by Lynne Langfeld

The Almanac by Lia Leendertz

The Hedgerow Handbook by Adele Nozedar

The Nature Seed by Lucy Jones and Kenneth Greenway

Wild Colour by Jenny Dean

INSTAGRAM

Christine Lewis @christinelewisstudio

Dose of Nature @dose_of_nature_

Hollie de cruz @theyesmummum

India Flint @prophet_of_bloom

Kathryn Davey @kathryn_davey

Pom Pom Factory @pompomfactory

Rebecca Desnos @rebeccadesnos

Suzi McLaughlin @suzimclaughlin

Tiffanie Turner @tiffanieturner

Zeena Shah @heartzeena

CRAFT MATERIALS

I usually start by checking Baker Ross, Hobbycraft or Jackson's online, but here are some tips for specific materials that may be a bit harder to source.

Edible flowers
finefoodspecialist.co.uk

Essential oils
essenceandalchemy.co.uk

Fabric dye powder (non-toxic)
ritdye.com

Fabric squares for crafting
om-baby.co.uk

Florists' wire
floristrywarehouse.com

Origami paper (lightweight)
thejapaneseshop.co.uk

Paints (outdoor acrylic)
arteza.co.uk

Silk handkerchief
silkcraft.co.uk

Soap
Liquid soap: drbronner.co.uk
Melt and Pour soap: cosyowl.com
or thesoapkitchen.co.uk

Wax pellets (soy or beeswax)
cosyowl.com

Index

About Laura

Laura Brand is an author and illustrator. She shares her crafty experiments and creative ideas for everyday play in her *Sunday Times* bestselling book *The Joy Journal for Magical Everyday Play* and on her online platform The Joy Journal. She has led workshops for children and adults at Fearne Cotton's Happy Place Festival, Port Eliot Festival and others.

Laura lives in the countryside with her husband, their two daughters, two dogs, ten cats and chickens. Home is a place of muddy boots, half-finished creative projects and DIY decorations. With chaos and calm in equal measure, Laura aspires to guide people in joyful crafting and a connection to nature that is accessible to all.

Laura has discovered that having her own creative outlet positively impacts her mental health and well-being and provides a welcome tonic in a busy world.

Instagram @thejoyjournal